# Contents

Contents

# Introduction

Speech and language difficulties affect children's social, emotional and educational development. Moreover, they are 'the most common neuro-developmental problem of childhood' (Goodyer, 2000). Estimates of the numbers of children affected vary depending on the definition criteria used. The situation is further complicated by the array of different terminology (for example, speech and language disorder, impairment or delay; developmental dysphasia or aphasia), but research studies suggest figures ranging from 5 to 7 per cent. This means that every class may have one or two children who need special consideration because of difficulty in understanding or using speech and language.

The purpose of this book is to help teachers identify and support children who have speech and language difficulties. If they are to be successfully included and given fair and equal access to the curriculum, a suitable communication environment is absolutely critical. To make inclusion a reality, differentiation strategies must be consistently applied. Unlike a child in a wheelchair or a child who has hearing aids, the child with a speech and language difficulty provides no immediate visual reminders of their disability. Such a child is dependent on the adults around modifying their language and expectations if they are to acquire the necessary independence skills to make their needs known.

The identification of speech and language difficulties can be a complex process. The key to success is close and informed observation based on knowledge of what might normally be expected of a child at a particular age and stage of development. The Afasic Checklists provide a structured approach to observation and a reliable basis for decision making about the further assessment that may be needed.

The support strategies described in this book are designed for implementation in mainstream classrooms but could also be used in a special school or language unit setting. Activities are suitable both for small groups and for a whole class (sometimes with modification). Many strategies can be used in a class where the teacher is the only adult, but the availability of a second adult (a teaching assistant, for example) will help with implementation of some suggestions.

## Who will benefit from this book?

This book has been written for teachers who work with children aged 4–10 years. It will be useful for class teachers, SENCos and specialist teachers and will also be of interest to heads and teaching assistants. The aim is to provide clear guidelines for identifying children who have speech and language difficulties and practical advice about how to support them. The emphasis throughout is on both the importance of multi-disciplinary working and the vital role of the teacher in the classroom in enabling these children to access the curriculum.

# Chapter 1
# What are speech and language difficulties?

Any child whose speech or language skills have not developed to the level expected for their chronological age may be described as having speech and language difficulties.

Speech and language difficulties are associated with a broad range of developmental conditions, including:

- learning disability;
- hearing impairment;
- physical disability (e.g. cerebral palsy);
- structural abnormality (e.g. cleft palate);
- autistic spectrum disorder.

In a very small number of cases, speech and language difficulties may be present as a result of physical, emotional or sexual abuse.

Usually a distinction is made between children who have speech and language difficulties in association with other developmental conditions and those whose development in other areas is broadly typical for their age but whose speech and language are not. The latter group are sometimes referred to as having 'specific' speech and language difficulties.

This book is written with children who have 'specific' speech and language difficulties in mind, but the principles of collaborative working apply to all children and the ideas for support may also be appropriate for children who have a range of developmental needs.

## A note about terminology

The literature on speech and language difficulties uses a wide range of terminology. Here is some you may have come across:

- specific language impairment;
- speech/language disorder;
- speech/language delay;
- developmental speech and language problems;
- speech, language and communication needs.

There are also diagnostic terms like 'dyspraxia' and 'phonological disorder' (see Glossary).

*'Children may have speech and language difficulties in one or more of several areas'*

In this book, 'speech and language difficulties' is used as a generic term to describe speech and language skills that are not as expected for a child's age or developmental level.

Children may have speech and language difficulties in one or more of several areas and the difficulties may range from mild to severe. The need for educational support will depend on the severity, the complexity and the persistence of the difficulties.

## Areas of difficulty

### *Speech*

Perhaps the most easily identified area of difficulty is production of speech. The child may not use certain sounds in their speech, which may affect their intelligibility. Errors to look out for include:

- consistent substitution of one sound for another – e.g. 't' for 's', so 'sun' becomes 'tun' and 'sand' becomes 'tand';
- problems with cluster production – e.g. 'bridge' becomes 'bidge', 'spoon' becomes 'poon' and 'plate' becomes 'pate';
- persistent problems with intelligibility or 'jumbled' speech.

Note that the use of 'f' for 'th' in the absence of other concerns is not a reason to refer to speech and language therapy. It does not affect the child's intelligibility and is also a feature of some dialects.

### *Receptive language*

The child with receptive language problems will have difficulty in understanding spoken language at the level expected for their age. Identification of receptive language difficulties in school-age children is not always easy because most children are adept at using visual and contextual cues to support their understanding of what is being said (this is part of the normal developmental process in acquiring comprehension skills). The problems arise when the language complexity outstrips this support, as might happen when the demands of the curriculum increase. Points to look out for include:

- difficulty in following instructions;
- expressive language difficulties (especially if severe or persistent);
- attention problems, especially in large group situations;
- difficulty in answering questions;
- behaviour problems;
- misunderstanding of written language.

### *Expressive language*

A child may have difficulty with putting words together in a sentence, with using grammatical structures and with vocabulary development. Points to look out for include:

- omitting parts of sentences, especially the small function words such as **the** and **is**, or grammatical markers on the ends of words such as **ing**;
- persistent errors with tense marking – e.g. **buyed** for **bought**;
- limited vocabulary development and difficulty in learning and remembering new words;
- word-finding problems – this may present as getting 'stuck for words', even with familiar vocabulary, or misnaming things (e.g. **knife** for **fork**, **tiger** for **lion**) or frequent use of non-specific labels such as **thingy** or **stuff**.

## *Pragmatics*

Pragmatics refers to the social use of language. It relates to the way in which we use language in interaction with other people, together with our understanding of the verbal and non-verbal rules that govern that process. Many children who have speech and language difficulties can be described as pragmatically immature. This will be evident in their play and social relationships.

There is a distinction, however, between a child who is pragmatically immature and one who has 'disordered pragmatic development'. The latter somehow 'feels' quite different, and involves abnormal or qualitatively different use and understanding of both verbal and non-verbal interaction. Disordered pragmatic development is sometimes seen in children who have autistic spectrum disorders. Points to look out for include:

- under-use or over-use of eye contact in supporting communication;
- difficulty in turn taking in conversation;
- unusual or 'single style' intonation or volume;
- over-use of stereotypical phrases including rather adult language or language borrowed from films or videos;
- lack of flexibility in thinking and interaction;
- difficulty in understanding and using tones of voice, gesture and facial expression;
- persistent difficulties in establishing peer relationships and managing in the playground.

## *Other communication difficulties*

There are other difficulties affecting a child's ability to communicate which may require referral for speech and language therapy assessment. These are not within the scope of this book, but it is important that teachers are aware of them because they can significantly affect children's communication and, in the case of non-fluency, seriously damage confidence and self-esteem.

### Disorders of fluency

Children may have mild to severe difficulties in producing fluent, smooth speech. These problems are sometimes referred to as stammering or stuttering. Speech and language therapists can offer assessment, treatment and advice on how best to give support.

### Voice disorders

A small number of children have a persistently hoarse or husky voice, which may require medical assessment. After being seen by an ENT consultant, they may have input from a speech and language therapist. As with other areas of difficulty, if a teacher has concerns about a particular child, these should be discussed with the child's parents.

## Associated difficulties

Speech and language difficulties are often associated with other difficulties, which will also affect the child's educational progress.

### *Motor difficulties*

Children may have fine or gross motor problems affecting a range of activities including handwriting, ball skills and PE generally, and self-help skills like dressing.

### *Behaviour difficulties*

Children may show a range of inappropriate behaviour, from low-level frustration and irritation to full-blown tantrums and physical aggression. It is advisable to consider the language skills of any child who is showing inappropriate behaviour.

### *Attention deficit*

Many children who have speech and language difficulties are also fidgety and easily distractible, and have a short attention span.

### *Social and emotional difficulties*

Children may be immature in their social and emotional development. They may also lack confidence and have poor self-esteem because of their communication difficulties.

## Why do children have speech and language difficulties?

The causes of specific speech and language difficulties have not yet been definitively identified, but genetic factors affecting brain development are certainly a likely cause for some children. The evidence for this comes from studies showing that speech, language and literacy difficulties may occur in several people from the same family (Byers Brown and Edwards, 1989). Other factors such as pre-natal infections and early brain damage have been suggested but, to date, have not been supported by convincing evidence (Bishop, 1992).

# Chapter 2 Identifying children with speech and language difficulties

## When is the best time to identify speech and language difficulties?

Many children who have speech and language difficulties are identified before they go to school. They may be seen by a variety of professionals. One typical route would be referral to the speech and language therapist by their health visitor after concerns being raised during a routine developmental check. If difficulties are present, parents are often aware that speech and language are not developing as they should by the time the child reaches 2 years of age. Although delayed language at 2 may not indicate a significant problem, parental concern should always be acted upon.

POINTERS

**Early referral**

Early referral enables the therapist to:

- diagnose any difficulty;
- engage multi-professional input;
- support and advise parents;
- plan for the child's education;
- monitor progress.

Clearly the potential benefits of early referral for the child are significant; it can ensure that they do not miss out at vital developmental stages, that they can access education from the moment of starting at school, and that 'bad' or 'unacceptable' behaviour resulting from their difficulty is given a correct interpretation and an appropriate response.

In spite of the recognised benefits of early identification (Cantwell and Baker, 1987), many children are not referred as pre-schoolers and they may be at nursery or in school before concerns are raised. There are many reasons why this happens:

- Parents may not have accessed pre-school services; they may not have realised that the child has difficulties or they may have been unable to attend routine clinic appointments.
- The child's language may have been good enough for them to manage at home with family and friends, but not to cope with the demands and expectations of school life.
- The child's difficulties may be quite subtle (especially with comprehension problems) and so not identified in the familiar context of home.
- A child who was identified earlier as 'delayed but progressing normally' may have become 'stuck', so that the gap between the speech and language skills they have and skills expected has begun to widen.

### *What should teachers look for?*

Once a child enters school, their best chance of having any previously unrecognised difficulties identified is through the skills and expertise of their class teacher. For some of these children, the first signs of difficulty with language may be poor educational progress or the emergence of behavioural problems. Often, it is only at this point that they are referred for speech and language therapy and found to have significant difficulties. Their problems are typically found to be in comprehension or phonological processing skills. Again, their language skills may be 'good enough' until they reach a stage where the language of the curriculum becomes more demanding, or until their peers move into the next stage of social development. Their fragile speech and language skills are no longer sufficient to enable them to cope educationally or socially and they start to struggle in the classroom or the playground.

*'Speech and language difficulties can be subtle and do not always present themselves in obvious ways'*

Because speech and language difficulties can be subtle and do not always present themselves in obvious ways, the decision to refer a child for speech and language therapy assessment may not always be an easy one for the class teacher. The Afasic Checklists (see pages 13–20) are designed for teachers to use with any child whom they suspect may have difficulties with speech and language development and who has not previously been identified. They provide a sound basis for deciding whether or not to refer the child for an assessment as well as for beginning to plan the kind of support that may be helpful to the child.

## Using the Afasic Checklists

The Afasic Checklists provide a reliable and valid means of identifying children who have speech and language difficulties. (Brief details of the research on which the checklists are based can be found in the Appendix.) The benefits of using such checklists lie not only in helping to decide which children might be referred for speech and language therapy assessment but also in the process itself:

- It allows you to focus on the child's communication skills in a semi-structured way. This immediately starts the process of differentiation and support, drawing on your expertise and experience in working with children who have difficulties.
- It provides information about the child's speech and language skills collected informally over a period of weeks or months. This is a valuable complement to the 'short, sharp' formal initial assessment carried out by the speech and language therapist. It also provides a picture of the child when relaxed in a familiar situation.
- It can facilitate discussion with parents about the child's difficulties. If you are making a referral, you will need to discuss it with the parents prior to sending the information to the speech and language therapy service. The checklist information can help in offering clear examples of difficulties seen in school and explaining why referral is needed. It can also help the therapist when they take the case history and are asking parents about their views and any corresponding difficulties seen at home.

Using the checklists requires no specialist training, equipment or resources.

It is important that you have regular contact with the child you are testing. It would be inappropriate to use a checklist with a child who has only recently started school or just joined a class. There are two checklists, one for use with 4- to 5-year-olds and the other for use with 6- to 10-year-olds.

Routine screening of whole classes should be carried out only with great caution and in discussion with the speech and language therapy service. It can be useful for specific purposes but those should be agreed before screening is carried out.

## *Checklist 4–5*

Checklist 4–5 is a milestone checklist; the items to be checked indicate normal development and the emphasis is on what the child can do. The checklist is divided into three main sections:

① Language structure
- Sound articulation
- Grammar

② Language content
- Attention and comprehension
- Vocabulary and expressive language

③ Ability to communicate
- One-to-one situation (with an adult)
- Group situation (with peers).

## *Checklist 6–10*

Checklist 6–10 is a 'problems' checklist; it focuses on behaviour in an older child that may indicate impaired speech and language development and the emphasis is on what the child *cannot* do. The checklist is divided into eight main sections:

① Response to sound
② Movement and motor skills
③ Cognitive processes
④ Errors in sound
⑤ Communication
⑥ Play and recreation
⑦ Vocabulary
⑧ Grammar.

*'Speech and language difficulties do not develop in isolation but in conjunction with other aspects of development.'*

Speech and language abilities do not develop in isolation but in conjunction with other aspects of development. By the inclusion of sections such as movement and motor skills, communication and cognitive processes, the checklists enable you to gain a more complete picture of a child's speech and language abilities.

## *How to use the checklists*

① Choose and copy the checklist relevant to the age of the child.
② Work through the list, deciding whether each item applies to the child you are testing. If it does, tick the box; if it does not, or if there is some doubt, leave the box empty.
③ When you have completed each section, add up the total for that section.
④ When you have completed the checklist, add together all the section scores and record the total score on the summary sheet.

## *Interpreting the results*

### Checklist 4–5

The maximum total score in checklist 4–5 is 50. A high score indicates normal or expected development and a low score indicates that a child's speech and language abilities are not developing as might be expected. Your decision for referral should be on the basis of two cut-off scores.

It is recommended that if a child scores less than 36 overall and/or less than 6 on the sound articulation subsection, you should refer them to speech and language therapy services for assessment, after discussion with the child's parents.

Children whose total score is less than 36 may have specific *language* difficulties; that is, they have no difficulty in the articulation or contrastive use of speech sounds but have some form of semantic or pragmatic impairment.

Children whose score on the sound articulation subsection is less than 6 may have specific *speech* difficulties such as dysfluency difficulties, physical difficulties in articulating sounds or phonological difficulties.

Children who score less than the cut-off in both the sound articulation subsection and the total score may have either phonological difficulties or any combination of articulation difficulties, phonological difficulties, receptive and expressive language difficulties, and pragmatic difficulties.

### Checklist 6–10

A high score in checklist 6–10 indicates impaired development and a low score indicates expected or normal development.

It is recommended that if a child's score is equal to or greater than 10, you should refer them to speech and language therapy services for assessment, after discussion with the child's parents.

## *What next?*

A child who reaches the cut-off score for a checklist should clearly be referred for further assessment. However, for some children who narrowly miss the cut-off scores, there may also be a case for referral – if, in your professional judgement, there is an over-riding concern that you feel the checklist does not address.

When a child does not meet the cut-off criteria, then the checklist profile, the subsection scores and the total scores are still useful in setting learning goals that are matched to the child's communicative abilities. Support strategies may still be required to tackle difficulties in a particular area. The table on pages 38–40 shows how the support strategies detailed in Chapter 4 relate to the areas highlighted by the checklist.

# Checklist 4–5

## Speech and language screening test for 4- to 5-year-olds

Child's name ______________________________

School ______________________________

Age ________ years ________ months Boy ☐ Girl ☐

First language ______________________________

Checklist completed by ______________________ Date ______________

Read each statement and decide whether or not it applies to the child. If it does, tick the box. If you are in any doubt, leave the box empty. At the end of each subsection add up the ticked boxes and enter the number as the subtotal.

## Summary

When you have completed all three sections, enter the totals for each section here. Add the section totals to calculate the total score.

Referral criterion cut-off

**1 Language structure**

Sound articulation ______ (5 or less)

Grammar ______

SECTION TOTAL ______

**2 Language content**

Attention and comprehension ______

Vocabulary and expressive language ______

SECTION TOTAL ______

**3 Ability to communicate**

One-to-one situation ______

Group situation ______

SECTION TOTAL ______

TOTAL SCORE ______ (35 or less)

REFERRAL/RECOMMENDATION ______________________________

______________________________

______________________________

______________________________

# Checklist 4–5

## 1 Language structure

### Sound articulation

a) Speech is clear and intelligible ☐

b) Speech is intelligible when child is excited or attempting a lengthy utterance ☐

c) Uses appropriate volume patterns when speaking, does not speak too loudly or softly ☐

d) Uses appropriate intonation to convey meaning
e.g. 'but *he* hit me' and '*Why* can't I?' ☐

e) Articulates simple words in full, does not omit initial or final consonant
e.g. '**y**ellow', 'be**d**', '**b**us' ☐

f) Articulates initial consonant clusters 'tr', 'pl', 'sp', 'sn'
e.g. '**tr**ain', '**pl**ane', '**sp**oon', '**sn**ake' ☐

g) Articulates final consonant clusters 'ng', 'mp', 'nk'
e.g. 'si**ng**', 'la**mp**', 'pi**nk**' ☐

h) Able to articulate multi-syllabic words in full, does not omit syllables
e.g. 'elephant', 'tomato', 'banana' ☐

SUBTOTAL ______

### Grammar

a) Uses determiners **the, a**
e.g. 'she has **a** dog' ☐

b) Uses conjunctions to link sentences
e.g. **and, when, because** ☐

c) Uses the correct regular and irregular present tense
e.g. 'he is running', 'she catches' ☐

d) Uses the correct regular and irregular past tense
e.g. 'she walked', 'it broke' ☐

e) Uses plurals correctly
e.g. **houses, men** ☐

f) Uses possessives
e.g. **Mum's car** ☐

g) Uses negative auxiliaries
e.g. **can't, won't, don't** ☐

h) Uses **what, who, where** to ask questions
e.g. '**Where** is Daddy?' ☐

SUBTOTAL ______

SECTION TOTAL ______

# Checklist 4–5

## 2 Language content

### Attention and comprehension

a) Able to attend to stimuli from two different sources e.g. completing a jigsaw and listening to the teacher ☐

b) Listens attentively to a simple story ☐

c) Able to follow stories unaccompanied by pictures ☐

d) Able to follow simple instructions e.g. 'Pick up the book and take it to the other room.' ☐

e) Understands the spatial concepts: **in, on, under** ☐

f) Understands words relating to time e.g. **yesterday, tomorrow, this afternoon** ☐

g) Understands emotion words e.g. **happy, sad, angry** ☐

h) Able to classify objects into categories e.g. types of fruit or animal ☐

SUBTOTAL ______

### Vocabulary and expressive language

a) Has wide vocabulary of basic words ☐

b) Is able to name shapes e.g. **square, circle, triangle** ☐

c) Is able to name sizes e.g. **big, small, tall, short** ☐

d) Uses comparatives e.g. **bigger, smaller, taller, shorter** ☐

e) Uses adverbs e.g. **quickly, slowly, loudly, quietly** ☐

f) Uses appropriate pronouns e.g. **I, me, my, mine, you, yours, your** ☐

g) Is able to summarise the content of stories ☐

h) Is able to describe a sequence of events e.g. 'They had a bath and then went to bed.' ☐

SUBTOTAL ______

SECTION TOTAL ______

# Checklist 4–5

## 3 Ability to communicate

| | One-to-one situation (with an adult) | Group situation (with peers) |
|---|---|---|
| a) Is willing to take part in conversations | ❑ | ❑ |
| b) Takes turns in conversations | ❑ | ❑ |
| c) Uses non-verbal devices to gain attention e.g. eye contact, physical contact | ❑ | ❑ |
| d) Uses non-verbal devices when listening e.g. assumes attentive body posture, maintains eye contact | ❑ | ❑ |
| e) Uses non-verbal devices when talking e.g. uses gestures, points, changes facial expression | ❑ | ❑ |
| f) Understands other people's non-verbal expressions and gestures | ❑ | ❑ |
| g) Uses verbal devices to gain attention e.g. **hey**, **look**, **see** | ❑ | ❑ |
| h) Initiates conversation e.g. by asking questions or making requests | ❑ | ❑ |
| i) Responds appropriately to questions and requests | ❑ | ❑ |
| SUBTOTAL | ______ | ______ |
| SECTION TOTAL | ______ | |

# Checklist 6–10

## Speech and language screening test for 6- to 10-year-olds

Child's name ______________________________

School ______________________________

Age ________ years ________ months Boy ☐ Girl ☐

First language ______________________________

Checklist completed by ______________________ Date ______________

Read each statement and decide whether or not it applies to the child. If it does, tick the box. If you are in any doubt, leave the box empty. At the end of each subsection add up the ticked boxes and enter the number as the subtotal.

## Summary

When you have completed all eight sections, enter the totals for each section here. Add the section totals to calculate the total score.

| | | SECTION TOTAL | Referral criterion cut-off |
|---|---|---|---|
| 1 | Response to sound | ______ | |
| 2 | Movement and motor skills | ______ | |
| 3 | Cognitive processes | ______ | |
| 4 | Errors in sound | ______ | |
| 5 | Communication | ______ | |
| 6 | Play and recreation | ______ | |
| 7 | Vocabulary | ______ | |
| 8 | Grammar | | |
| | TOTAL SCORE | ______ | (10 or less) |

REFERRAL/RECOMMENDATION ______________________________

______________________________

______________________________

______________________________

______________________________

# Checklist 6–10

## 1 Response to sound

a) Shows confusion between vowels, consonants, and consonant clusters, leading to difficulty in learning phonics and word-attack skills .................. ☐

b) Cannot imitate a simple handclap rhythm .................................................................. ☐

c) Has difficulty in recognising simple tunes .................................................................. ☐

d) Has difficulty in discriminating pitch .................................................................. ☐

e) Has difficulty in screening out irrelevant sounds and attending to verbal information e.g. when the teacher is talking .................................................. ☐

SECTION TOTAL ______

## 2 Movement and motor skills

a) Finds judging speed and distance difficult e.g. when catching a ball .................................................. ☐

b) Has not established a preference for the right or left hand or the right or left foot .................................................................. ☐

c) Has poorly developed self-help skills e.g. has problems with dressing, eating, washing .............................. ☐

d) Has poor pencil control .................................................................. ☐

e) Has poor co-ordination e.g. finds it difficult to use alternate feet when walking downstairs, to hop on one foot or to kick a ball .................................................. ☐

SECTION TOTAL ______

## 3 Cognitive processes

a) Has difficulty in understanding the language of sequencing e.g. **before, after** .................................................. ☐

b) Has difficulty in ordering a sequence of activities required to complete a task e.g. cooking .................................................. ☐

c) Has difficulty in learning the order of days of the week, months, seasons .................................................................. ☐

d) Has difficulty recalling three or more items in short-term memory .................................................................. ☐

e) Has poor verbal long-term memory for single words .................................................................. ☐

SECTION TOTAL ______

# Checklist 6–10

## 4 Errors in sound

a) Omits the beginnings and endings of words
e.g. 'pretending' becomes 'tending' . . . . . . . . . . . . . . . . . . . . . . . . . . . . . . . . . . . . . . . . . ☐

b) Reduces multi-syllabic words
e.g. 'potato' becomes 'tato' . . . . . . . . . . . . . . . . . . . . . . . . . . . . . . . . . . . . . . . . . . . . . . . ☐

c) Speaks less intelligibly when excited
. . . . . . . . . . . . . . . . . . . . . . . . . . . . . . . . . . . . . . . . . . . . . . . . . . . . . . . . . . . . . . . . . . ☐

d) Speaks less intelligibly when attempting a lengthy utterance
. . . . . . . . . . . . . . . . . . . . . . . . . . . . . . . . . . . . . . . . . . . . . . . . . . . . . . . . . . . . . . . . . . ☐

e) Shows persistent confusion between voiced and unvoiced sounds
e.g. **p/b, f/v, t/d, k/g** . . . . . . . . . . . . . . . . . . . . . . . . . . . . . . . . . . . . . . . . . . . . . . . . . . . ☐

SECTION TOTAL ______

## 5 Communication

a) Has delayed understanding of question words
e.g. **what, who** . . . . . . . . . . . . . . . . . . . . . . . . . . . . . . . . . . . . . . . . . . . . . . . . . . . . . . . ☐

b) Does not follow instructions without prompting
. . . . . . . . . . . . . . . . . . . . . . . . . . . . . . . . . . . . . . . . . . . . . . . . . . . . . . . . . . . . . . . . ☐

c) Offers limited verbal comments on own activities
. . . . . . . . . . . . . . . . . . . . . . . . . . . . . . . . . . . . . . . . . . . . . . . . . . . . . . . . . . . . . . . . ☐

d) Gives unexpected responses to questions
. . . . . . . . . . . . . . . . . . . . . . . . . . . . . . . . . . . . . . . . . . . . . . . . . . . . . . . . . . . . . . . . ☐

e) Uses inappropriate intonation and volume when speaking
. . . . . . . . . . . . . . . . . . . . . . . . . . . . . . . . . . . . . . . . . . . . . . . . . . . . . . . . . . . . . . . . ☐

SECTION TOTAL ______

## 6 Play and recreation

a) Has difficulty following a story without many visual cues
. . . . . . . . . . . . . . . . . . . . . . . . . . . . . . . . . . . . . . . . . . . . . . . . . . . . . . . . . . . . . . . . ☐

b) Has no play involving sounds, rhymes or words
. . . . . . . . . . . . . . . . . . . . . . . . . . . . . . . . . . . . . . . . . . . . . . . . . . . . . . . . . . . . . . . . ☐

c) Is slow to learn rules of group games and positions in sports
. . . . . . . . . . . . . . . . . . . . . . . . . . . . . . . . . . . . . . . . . . . . . . . . . . . . . . . . . . . . . . . . ☐

d) Enjoys the visual content of television programmes
but finds it hard to follow stories and plots . . . . . . . . . . . . . . . . . . . . . . . . . . . . . . . . ☐

e) Humour tends towards visual and slapstick with
poor appreciation of verbal jokes and puns . . . . . . . . . . . . . . . . . . . . . . . . . . . . . . . . ☐

SECTION TOTAL ______

## 7 Vocabulary

a) Has difficulty with words relating to time
e.g. **afternoon** ☐

b) Has difficulty with prepositions and adverbs ☐

c) Has difficulty with words that change their reference in different circumstances
e.g. **sister, daughter, here, there** ☐

d) Has frequent 'tip of the tongue' moments
i.e. is unable to recall words previously known ☐

e) Tends towards literal interpretation of idiom
e.g. 'pull your socks up' ☐

SECTION TOTAL ______

## 8 Grammar

a) Omits auxiliary verbs
e.g. 'I been shopping' (omitting **have**) ☐

b) Omits the verb **to be**
e.g. 'David naughty' (omitting **is**) ☐

c) Does not change word order to form questions
e.g. 'He is going?' instead of 'Is he going?' ☐

d) Omits word endings
e.g. in plurals or possessives ☐

e) Omits whole words
e.g. 'Where book?' (omitting **is the**) ☐

SECTION TOTAL ______

# Chapter 3
# Supporting roles

Assessment and support for children with speech and language difficulties comes from a variety of people with different but complementary roles to play. The key to success is good communication between all the people involved with an individual child, clarity about who has responsibility for what and a shared sense of what we are trying to achieve. It may not be possible for the child to achieve 'normal' speech and language but they can be helped to function to the best of their ability and be supported so they develop coping strategies and work towards independence.

The range of people involved with a child may vary depending on individual circumstances and needs and may also change over time. For example, many children will see an educational psychologist or a community paediatrician for an initial assessment, but most of the ongoing support will come from parents, school staff and the speech and language therapist.

*'The key to success is good communication between all the people involved with an individual child'*

The diagram gives a general overview of the structure of educational support provided by LEAs. The needs of many children will be met through the usual differentiated curriculum in the classroom or possibly with the extra help accessed through School Action or School Action Plus. Children with more severe difficulties may require statutory assessment and through that process be given a Statement of Special Educational Needs.

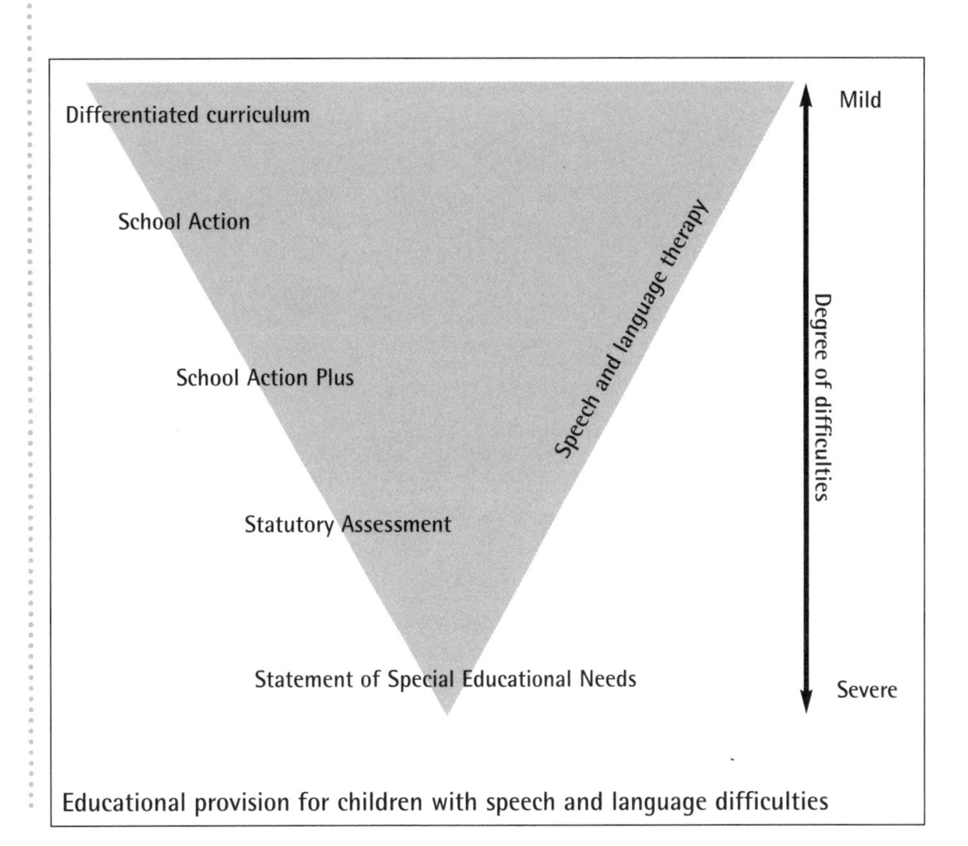


Educational provision for children with speech and language difficulties

Individual children clearly have different needs requiring different types of support. Although, as the diagram indicates, the provision made for an individual child will be largely determined by the severity and complexity of difficulties, it can also be influenced by other factors. These may include the child's temperament and coping strategies, parental attitudes and support, and the competence and confidence of the teaching staff.

Case study

### Sophie

After one term in Reception, Sophie's ability both to comprehend and to use language in a variety of situations was a cause of concern to her teacher and a source of frustration to her parents. Her score on the Afasic Checklist was 16. She was referred to speech and language therapy for assessment. This showed that she had difficulty with every aspect of language apart from her speech, which was clear.

Sophie was supported through School Action for a term and had speech and language therapy at the local clinic. Her increasing difficulty in the classroom, however, led to an early review of her IEP and the decision to go for statutory assessment.

Her SEN statement, given on the basis of severe language disorder, provided access to 15 hours a week of LSA time. The class teacher, the LSA, the SLT and her parents were all involved in planning a support package for her that included:

- visual support in all areas of the curriculum;
- use of a visual timetable;
- small-group vocabulary teaching;
- one-to-one speech and language therapy in school with her LSA to provide follow-up on specific concepts and language structures;
- a home-school book for communication between staff and parents.

## The speech and language therapist

### *Assessment*

Speech and language therapists (SLTs) are able to assess the child's speech, language and communication skills. This is done through:

- a detailed discussion with parents about the child's developmental history;
- use of formal standardised tests;
- observation of the child;
- use of informal assessment activities;
- information from other professionals who know the child.

### *Diagnosis and description of needs*

During assessment the SLT will decide whether or not the child's speech, language and communication skills are as expected for their age or whether they have difficulties in any of these areas. The idea of 'diagnosis' perhaps sits uncomfortably in an educational context, but it reflects the health service employment of SLTs. Diagnosis means that the SLT considers the child's different levels of communicative functioning (strengths as well as difficulties), the relationship between them and the impact of any difficulties on the child's ability to function at home and at school. This will lead to a description of the support the child needs.

The SLT will consider:

- what input is needed from the speech and language therapy service;
- what input is needed from school staff in relation to the child's speech and language difficulties;
- what input may come from the parents.

## *Therapy input*

Speech and language therapy services across the country currently offer very different models of input, but the types of provision that may be available are:

- one-to-one therapy on a continuous or block basis;
- group therapy, usually on a block basis, which may be weekly or intensive;
- advice to parents – this is always given following assessment but may also be the preferred method of input, either individually or in a group;
- advice to school staff (class teachers, teaching assistants and specialist teachers) – this may be at a one-to-one level or may include in-service training.

SLTs are able to discuss with teachers the likely impact of the child's speech and language difficulties in the classroom, both in general terms and in accessing the curriculum. There are two main approaches to support (which may operate together).

### 1. A programme targeting specific areas of difficulty

This can be incorporated into an individual education plan (IEP). It is often delivered in the classroom but may need to be via a one-to-one or small-group session with a teaching assistant. If, for example, a child needs to learn the pronouns **he** and **she**, it is unlikely that other children in the class will need to be taught these. Such a specific target might best be introduced in one-to-one sessions with opportunities for generalisation then being created in the classroom.

### 2. Specific strategies to support the child

When the child's difficulties have been clearly identified, there are a range of strategies that may be useful in giving support. To maximise the effectiveness of these strategies it is important that they are applied as consistently as possible. One of the keys to this is good forward planning. For example, an agreed strategy might be to introduce new topic vocabulary to the child before it is met in class. The child will therefore need to be given a session using, for example, visual materials to support the teaching prior to the whole-class lesson. Time and a teaching assistant will need to be allocated and suitable materials prepared.

There has been an increasing emphasis on the consultancy model of speech and language therapy, in which teachers and teaching assistants provide close support for individual children based on advice from SLTs or following programmes discussed and agreed between SLTs and school staff. In order for this approach to be effective, sufficient time must be given to discussion, focusing on the needs of the individual child. There has to be good communication between all those concerned as well as sufficient trust and understanding for everyone to identify their own skills and training needs in order to be able to work with the child.

Similarly, it is important to work towards a common understanding and agreement about which children need direct therapy input from an SLT, based not just on severity and complexity (although these are clearly important) but also on our developing understanding of 'what works best' for different types of speech and language difficulty. For some children a mixture of approaches will be needed and different types of input will be appropriate at different stages of their development.

### *Discharge*

When the SLT thinks that they no longer have a role with a child, they will, in consultation with the parents and the teacher, discharge the child from their support service. This can sometimes cause anxiety because the child may still have speech and language difficulties. The most common reasons for discharge are as follows:

- The child's speech and language skills are appropriate for their age.
- The child's speech and language skills are in line with other areas of their skills and general learning ability.
- The child is being effectively supported in the classroom and the SLT does not need to make any active contribution at the present time.
- The child is not benefiting from therapy input at the present time or there are no achievable goals to focus on.

A 'successful' discharge is one where:

- the process is planned and agreed in advance;
- the support strategies for the child (if still needed) are successfully in place and parents and school staff are confident about managing them;
- everyone is clear about how to re-refer the child and what might prompt a re-referral.

## The teacher

### *Identification*

All teachers need to be aware of the types of problem in learning and in behaviour that may indicate a child has speech and language difficulties. Teachers suspecting that a child may have difficulties should refer the child to the speech and language therapy service for an assessment. The use of the Afasic Checklists gives structure to observation and can help in deciding whether to make a referral as well as improving the quality of information given to support the referral (see Chapter 2).

### *Support*

Following assessment, whatever the approach taken for therapy input (see above), the SLT will work with the class teacher to ensure that they are able to give the child the support necessary in the classroom. The teacher will need to:

- be aware of the impact of speech, language and communication difficulties on the child's ability to access the curriculum;
- be able to differentiate appropriately within schemes of work and teaching plans, incorporating advice from the SLT when appropriate;
- identify clear teaching objectives;
- understand how to set achievable targets ('small steps') on an IEP;
- monitor progress;
- consistently apply the support strategies agreed for the child;
- ensure that the teaching assistant understands how to support the child appropriately;
- ensure that the teaching assistant has sufficient preparation time when needed;
- know when and how to contact the SLT.

## Heads and SENCos

Heads and SENCos will support the work of the class teacher and, if needed, guide them through the process of statutory assessment. SENCos will be involved from the outset in the identification of children with speech and language difficulties, in discussion with class teachers, and in advising on support strategies.

It is helpful if:

- there is general awareness in the school of the needs of children with speech and language difficulties (one of the largest identifiable groups of children with special educational needs (SEN) within a school population);
- heads and SENCos are aware of the levels of skill and knowledge of staff in relation to SEN, and of their possible training needs;
- staff are encouraged to access training if needed;
- the class teacher is given non-contact time to meet with the SLT for joint planning;
- the SLT and SENCo meet at least termly to discuss children's needs and to review joint working practices;
- suitable working space is available for the SLT when they come into school;
- the SLT is invited to annual reviews and IEP meetings as appropriate and given as much notice of dates as possible. (The SLT may not always be able to attend; but if given the information, can send in a report and arrange attendance at priority review meetings.)

## The teaching assistant

Assistance in the classroom may come in various forms and under various labels including classroom assistants (CAs), learning support assistants (LSAs) and special needs assistants (SNAs). Here, teaching assistant (TA) is used to denote any adult providing assistance to the class teacher.

The TA has a vital role in supporting children who have speech and language difficulties and in supporting the class teacher who is responsible for the day-to-day planning and the education of the child. The key to enabling the TA to provide effective support is, again, good communication. As the class teacher, you should try to ensure that they:

- are included in discussions involving the SLT and you, the class teacher;
- have the opportunity to discuss their training needs in relation to speech and language difficulties and are then able to access suitable training (ideally the TA and class teacher would attend training sessions together in order to maximise their benefits);
- contribute to a child's IEP and are familiar with the targets;
- have a clear understanding of the strategies, materials and methods needed to achieve the targets;
- understand how to help the generalisation of new skills;
- understand what to look for in monitoring progress;
- have non-contact time in order to prepare necessary materials;
- are able to find a balance between giving enough support and allowing the child to develop independence skills as appropriate; this is particularly (but not only) important in the area of the child's communication;
- are able to support home–school liaison, in agreement with the class teacher;
- know when and how to ask for help from the teacher and the SLT.

As part of the communication process, the TA will need to keep some kind of record of work. This can be quite simple, along the lines of the one here.

**Special Needs Weekly Record**

Week beginning: 24.01.02 Class: Rec. Children: Kirsty, Stephanie, Omar

| | Activities with LSA | LSA notes |
|---|---|---|
| Monday | 1. Categorising: clothes<br>2. Game: Give me something that … keeps your toes warm, etc.<br>3. Game with role reversal (children give clues) | 1. Did not know the names of all items of clothing<br>2. Good<br>3. All struggled with the idea of the game first time round. They said the name of the object rather than a clue. |
| Tuesday | 1. Syllables (1 + 3) | 1. Lots more work needed. All the children were unfamiliar with some of the objects and their uses. |
| Wednesday | | |
| Thursday | 1. Letter recognition: a, o, c, w, r, j | Session interrupted by the photographer. |
| Friday | 1. Story: The Little Red Hen (with James and Anya)<br>2. Letter recognition: a, o, c, w, r, j | 1. None of them had any ideas about 'looking for clues' about the book. All listened well but found retelling hard.<br>2. Some improvement on recognition but lots more work needed. |

Suggestions / requests for help / action

.................................................

.................................................

.................................................

It also helps if the TA is:

- calm;
- positive;
- consistent;
- and has a good sense of humour!

## The specialist teacher

The availability of specialist teachers may vary from place to place, and different LEAs have slightly different criteria for access. Some authorities refer to the specialist teacher when a child is at School Action Plus; others may stipulate access through statutory assessment. Whatever the access route, the role of specialist teacher may include the following elements:

- advice on strategies and target setting for the child;
- help in incorporating language targets into the curriculum;
- advice on classroom organisation and management;
- support for IEP and review meetings;
- contribution to the planning and review process;
- advice on record keeping;
- advice on progress monitoring;
- advice on teaching and learning styles;
- training for school staff;
- work with individual children on specific aspects of language – e.g. social skills, written language skills;
- support for children at educational transitions – e.g. from a language unit into mainstream school or primary to secondary transfer.

Liaison between the SLT and the specialist teacher is essential to maximise the benefits to the child and school staff of their related but different skills.

## Working together: teachers and therapists

To be effective in planning and delivering support for children who have speech and language difficulties, SLTs and teachers need to work together. The Special Educational Needs Code of Practice (2001) is clear: 'collaborative practice is essential for successful intervention with children and young people with speech and language difficulties'. Teachers and therapists will need little convincing of this ideal, but practicalities sometimes make the achievement of meaningful collaboration seem quite a challenge. The following approaches and strategies are useful to keep in mind as we work towards building effective working relationships.

### *Make time to talk*

Arranging a time suitable for both of you may require a little flexibility; a teacher can't always have non-contact time; a therapist may be available for the school only on a Tuesday morning, for example.

### Listen to each other

A child may behave very differently one-to-one and in a classroom. The differing perspectives we bring are vitally important in understanding the strengths and difficulties of an individual child. By being more aware of them, we can plan sensitive and effective support.

### Ask questions

It is easy to slip into using jargon or technical language and assume that other people will understand. It is also easy to listen to other people's jargon with only half an understanding of what it means. Ask questions and check out assumptions:

*'So, by 'phonology' you mean . . . '*

"He's stopping his fricatives and devoicing his plosives.....!!"

### Focus on the child

Teachers and speech therapists each have 'expert' knowledge of the child. By drawing on each other's knowledge you can support observations and information. At each stage, check that the plan really meets the child's needs.

### Don't believe the myths

Professional boundaries can sometimes get in the way of working effectively together and cause tension in relationships. We can foster good working relationships by being positive in our approaches to each other and by keeping the focus on the child's needs. For example:

*'Speech and language therapists never stay very long.'*

could be reframed as

*'I know the SLT service has had some recruitment difficulties but our last therapist was actually in post for two years. Our new SLT will welcome my support while she gets to know the school.'*

### Be realistic

In planning, aim for what is possible rather than what would be ideal but is probably impossible to achieve. Recognise the limitations (which are often due to working situations rather than lack of skills or knowledge) whilst not setting expectations too low. For example, a detailed and well-constructed language programme is no use at all if there is no time for an adult to work regularly on a one-to-one basis with the child. On the other hand, a relatively simple measure such as always remembering to check that the child has understood whole-class instructions may completely change their experience of success.

Be honest about what you can do and what you need or expect from those involved in different roles in order to support the child effectively.

### Be clear

Good communication underpins the relationship between the teacher and the SLT. A few simple measures will greatly increase the chances of a really effective collaboration:

- Summarise the end of each discussion with something like, 'Well, what we've agreed is . . . '

- Agree how actions will be recorded.
- Plan when the next meeting will take place.
- Check you know how to contact each other should the need arise.

And, of course, don't make promises you can't keep!

### *Talk to parents*

Parents need to know that you have met together and what has been agreed. Ideally, parents will be included in the discussion but for a variety of reasons this does not always happen. In that case you will need to agree who will feed back to parents and how. When SLTs and teachers jointly plan to meet a child's needs, parents generally feel more confident about the effectiveness of input for their child.

## Working together: professionals and parents

It should go without saying that parents are the most important people in the child's life and that the positive involvement of parents makes an enormous difference in the process of supporting the child successfully. Yet, parents may easily feel alienated and daunted when their child has difficulties and they are faced with having to deal with professionals. The SEN Code of Practice (2001) clearly describes key principles in communicating and working with parents. It says:

> Positive attitudes to parents, user-friendly information and procedures and awareness of support needs are important. There should be no presumption about what parents can or cannot do to support their child's learning. Stereotypic views of parents are unhelpful and should be challenged. All staff should bear in mind the pressures a parent may be under because of the child's needs.
>
> To make communications effective professionals should:
>
> - acknowledge and draw on parental knowledge and expertise in relation to their child;
> - focus on the children's strengths as well as areas of additional need;
> - recognise the personal and emotional investment of parents and be aware of their feelings;
> - ensure that parents understand procedures, are aware of how to access support in preparing their contributions, and are given documents to be discussed well before meetings;
> - respect the validity of differing perspectives and seek constructive ways of reconciling different viewpoints;
> - respect the differing needs parents themselves may have, such as a disability or communication and linguistic barriers;
> - recognise the need for flexibility in the timing and structure of meetings.

These principles apply to all parents, whatever the degree of difficulty the child has. Sometimes in the past, speech and language difficulties have been referred to as a 'hidden' difficulty and the 'hidden' nature of the child's disorder has led to parents feeling isolated and unsupported. Teachers and SLTs need to work together to support parents as well as children.

## Involving the child

We have an obligation to include children in decision making and to ensure that they have the opportunity to indicate choices and express their feelings. Articles 12 and 13 of the United Nations Convention on the Rights of the Child state these principles:

> Children, who are capable of forming views, have a right to receive and make known information, to express an opinion, and to have that opinion taken into account in any matters affecting them. The views of the child should be given due weight according to the age, maturity and capability of the child.

The SEN Code of Practice describes how children may be involved in the process of target setting and annual reviews. However, children with speech and language difficulties are in particular danger of being disadvantaged in this process and we need to consider how we facilitate the development of the skills needed to avoid that.

### *Equipping the child for involvement*

If children are to have the best chance of meaningful participation, we need to develop the skills needed from an early age. The skills are essentially those fostered through good social skills input and are they not wholly dependent on the level of the child's language, although clearly this will heavily influence their ability to understand and express what they want to say.

To be effective, strategies for developing the necessary skills of self-expression must be used at home and at school. Here are some ideas for developing the skills of self-expression in the classroom.

#### Making choices

- The child can be offered alternatives – e.g. 'Orange or blackcurrant?' or 'Coat or jumper?', or open-ended choices – e.g. 'What do you want to drink?' or 'What do you want to wear?'
- When appropriate, allow children to make group choices, by asking for a show of hands or using some other 'voting' system.
- Find a balance between giving models to children who need them (so they make a choice after hearing several other children have their turn) and sometimes insisting that they go first (thereby having to make a real choice rather than copying someone else).

#### Expressing opinions

- To practise expressing likes and dislikes, play games such as My Favourite Thing, passing a beanbag round a circle and taking turns to say 'My favourite colour is . . . ' or 'My favourite animal is . . . '.
- Play Fact and Opinion (or Thumbs Up). Take turns to make a statement, e.g. 'Football is boring!' Everyone puts their thumbs up if they agree, thumbs down if they disagree and thumbs in a neutral middle position if they neither agree nor disagree. The aim is to show that it is acceptable for people to have different opinions and that they have the right to be heard.

- Encourage children to express views about moral issues using stories as a basis for discussion. (The opportunity for this may arise naturally in literacy, history or RE sessions.) If they have difficulty in explaining, e.g., why something is right or wrong, giving several options as a starting point for discussion can be helpful.

*'Allow the child to experience the power of effective communication'*

### Experiencing effective communication

Allow the child to experience the power of effective communication (something rarely experienced by some children). They can:

- give instructions to other children, supported as needed – e.g. using an obstacle course in PE sessions, choosing what to sing in music;
- take turns to choose a game to play at playtime;
- take a message to another class (with you having prepared the other teacher if necessary).

### Experiencing responsibility

Give the child a responsibility. This must be something 'real' that genuinely needs to be done. For example they can:

- take the register to the school office;
- turn the music player on and off at the beginning and end of assembly;
- give out or collect worksheets;
- care for the class plants or pets.

### Time to talk

- Make a regular time for talking, e.g. weekend news or Circle Time. The child with speech and language difficulties will need extra time which is not pressured in which their contributions can be acknowledged and shown to be valued.
- Do a 'story circle' in which everyone takes turns to add a sentence to a story (either written or verbal). This works best in a small group so that no-one has to wait too long for their next turn.
- Have children working in pairs to write or tell a story or to describe a science experiment or school trip. The topic can be anything that allows for equal turns and encourages use of language. Give the children props if necessary to help them recall and structure the piece. They record their work either by using a tape recorder or having one of the pair act as a scribe.

### Role play

This could cover a range of topics, for example retelling or acting out a story, role playing social situations in the classroom or the playground, or practising 'scripts' for situations which the child may need to deal with (e.g. being involved in your annual review). The child may need lots of practice to feel confident with a situation. Structured opportunities to carry over skills into real-life situations may also need to be provided. If the situation is one in which the child needs to express their own thoughts and ideas, you will need extra preparation time to help them with this aspect before incorporating them into a role play.

## Feelings and emotions

Some children with speech and language difficulties may find it hard to use emotion words and to understand what they mean. The following strategies may be helpful:

- Use visual cue cards to represent common emotion words, e.g. **happy**, **sad**, **angry**, **worried**, **bored**. Play a guessing game with children, in which they take turns to act out an emotion.
- Talk about how you can guess how someone is feeling (facial expression, body language, tone of voice) and how this links to physical sensations (how you feel inside). Apply this to characters in stories, children's news or things that happen in the playground.
- As the child develops skills in recognising and labelling emotions, introduce more advanced emotion words such as **curious**, **miserable**, **cheerful**, **glum**.
- Use stories and topic work to help generalise the child's understanding and use of this vocabulary.

## Evaluating own work

If the child is to be involved in target setting and in monitoring their own progress, they need to be given experience in assessing their own performance on tasks, together with lots of encouragement and support:

- Give the child a frame of reference for assessing their performance, asking, e.g., how well they organised getting started. Did they understand what they had to do? (And if not, what did they do about that?) Have they finished the task? Is it their best writing? Alternatively, there might be just one thing the child has to evaluate, but this must be done consistently.
- If the child makes negative comments about their work, encourage them to say something positive as well (when appropriate).
- Make positive comparisons between children's work, e.g. 'Ryan's dinosaur looks really fierce, I like his sharp teeth; and Thomas has drawn a huge brontosaurus, look at his lovely long neck.'

## Talking about their speech and language difficulties

We need to discuss with parents how we talk to the child about their strengths and difficulties and about why they sometimes need extra or different help. Children vary in their awareness and in when they recognise that certain things are difficult for them. Clearly we need to be sensitive to this and we need to begin to discuss the issues at a suitable point. In this way we can help children develop a positive conceptual framework for how they see themselves both at home and at school.

# Chapter 4
# Strategies for support

In thinking about support strategies for the child with speech and language difficulties, there are two strands to consider. First, there is a range of general ideas that will be useful for any child with these difficulties. These include considerations such as what a child might need to function within a class environment and how best to deliver vital information. Then there are specific strategies linked to specific problems such as those identified using the Afasic Checklists.

*'Successful support is achieved through planning, time and consistency and through carefully thought-through targets designed for each individual child.'*

Successful support is achieved through planning, time and consistency and through carefully thought-through targets designed for each individual child. Of course, this is not to say that children's needs cannot be met in a group – indeed, group work is essential for children's development – but the adult running the group must be aware of each child's individual needs.

## General support

This section focuses on the first strand: general strategies that will help a wide range of children.

### *Support in the classroom*

Giving some thought to classroom organisation and planning for regular routines can make a significant difference to the smooth running of the day and ensure that the child feels comfortable within a familiar structure. The following ideas may help the child who is struggling to manage classroom life:

- The child will probably find it helpful to sit near you at the front of the class.
- Teach the child to be alert for stock phrases such as 'I want everyone to listen.' Explain to all the children what this means, e.g., 'When you hear this it means "Pencils down, arms folded, looking at me."' The child with speech and language difficulties may need extra help to realise that they are required to listen and focus on what you are saying.
- When you are talking to the class as a whole, try to keep background noise to a minimum. (Open-plan classrooms can be especially difficult for the child because of the noise.)
- If possible, create a quiet area in the classroom for small-group activities, in which the child can take time out if they need it. Children with speech and language difficulties can become very tired from the effort they need to put in to attend, to listen and to process language.
- If the class is sitting on the carpet, ensure the child is at the front next to you.
- Plan ahead. You will know whether or not the child is likely to encounter problems in any given session. How will you modify activities or expectations to ensure that they succeed?
- If there is more than one adult in the classroom, maximise the benefit, again by planning ahead. For example if a TA is available to support the child,

| Benjamin | Year 1 |
|---|---|
| PE: needs supervision in getting changed but is otherwise independent | |
| Literacy: needs a teaching assistant next to him throughout the session to help with reading and recording | |
| Art: needs help to organise materials but is otherwise independent | |
| Maths: needs help in organising support apparatus, a reminder about writing numbers and help to get started on a task. If the task is familiar, then just needs periodic checks. If a new concept has been introduced, needs an adult with him | |

decide in advance what needs to be done in each session. It may help to have a general plan, outlining the different types of support needed in different curriculum areas.

- Be aware of particular times of the day that may cause difficulties, e.g., transition times. The child may be confused by a change of task, bump into others if many children are moving around at the same time, forget what they are doing or be unable to organise what they need for the next session. Unexpected events (e.g. losing a lunch box, wet play) can cause upset or frustration. The key to success is, again, good planning.
- The child may need help in developing organisational and study skills. It can be helpful to use cue cards for different sessions.

## *Processing information*

Children with speech and language difficulties are often slow or inefficient in processing auditory information. They take time to work through instructions and information and take longer to respond to questions than most children. In situations where there are distractions or high levels of background noise, this can be even more difficult. If children feel under pressure to respond quickly they may become anxious, which only exacerbates the problem.

We can help the child in a variety of ways. At first sight some of the following suggestions may appear to require extra adult time, but they may actually save time overall by reducing the need for repetition and by enhancing the child's learning opportunities.

- Ensure you have the child's attention before starting to talk. Remember, saying 'everybody' does not necessarily alert the child to the fact that you mean them as well. You may need to say that child's name and make sure they are looking at you.
- Reduce background noise wherever possible.
- Talk slowly and clearly but with normal intonation and emphasis.
- You may consider slightly raising the volume of your voice (but you don't need to shout). Make sure you are not straining your voice.
- When possible, give the child early warning of what might be happening next, e.g. 'In 5 minutes we will be stopping our writing and getting changed for PE.'
- 'Chunk' information into natural pieces; leave a pause after each chunk to allow the child time to process what you have said.
- Summarise key points at suitable intervals and support this with visual information.
- Check that key points have been understood before moving on to the next task. You could ask the whole class or check with the child individually as you move on.
- When asking questions you may find the child needs extra time to respond. Sometimes a helpful rule of thumb is to ask the question, count up to ten silently, wait a bit longer, and then ask if they would like you to say it again. Rephrasing helps some children but for others it is confusing because they

think you are asking another, different question. Waiting for a response can sometimes feel like a long time and we tend to get rather embarrassed for the child. Clearly we need to manage it with sensitivity, but the silence does give the child processing space and as you both become used to dealing with the problem in this way it will feel more natural.

- Talk with the child about what they find most helpful. With older children especially, this is an important way of establishing a 'working partnership'.
- Whatever strategies you use one-to-one with the child will also apply in whole-class situations. For example, when the child puts their hand up to answer a question, they will sometimes need a long time to respond. This may need to be discussed with all the children – e.g., 'Sometimes we all need extra thinking time. In this class we wait quietly for people to answer questions when it's their turn. We stay quiet and still while they are thinking.'

## *Visual support*

We frequently talk about providing 'visual support' for children with speech and language difficulties. This can take many forms depending on the age and stage of the child, the curriculum area and the availability of materials. The purpose is to aid the child's understanding of what is being talked about, to provide extra information, to help 'fix' new concepts and vocabulary, and to be a tangible reminder of what has been talked about after the spoken word is gone. Here are just a few ideas.

### Real objects

Allow children to hold them and feel their weight and texture. Get them to repeat the name of an object whilst holding it.

### Pictures

Ensure that children know which part of the picture you are referring to. Consider the complexity of the picture. Specific information can support their understanding of what is being said, but some beautifully illustrated children's books are too complex for children to be able to focus on. Children's own drawings or paintings may be useful as an immediate aid but less so over time for young children whose pictures are necessarily immature.

### Photos

Taking photographs in the classroom can be enormously helpful as a record of what was done and to help children recall vocabulary and events.

### Video

Unfortunately, use of a video camera is not always a practical proposition, but making a video recording of an event or teaching session and allowing the child to see it again (ideally with an adult to stop the video and talk about salient features) can be very useful. Videos 'starring' the child and their classmates are particularly powerful, but the experience may need to become a familiar one before you can really take advantage of learning opportunities (as the novelty of being on video becomes less distracting).

A Rebus sentence

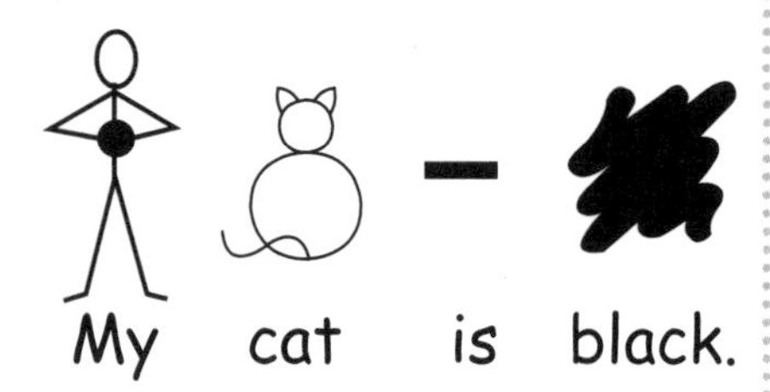


### Written materials and symbols

Written support, presented in a clear format, can help, especially where key words and simple language are used. For non-readers, little pictures or a set of recognised symbols (such as Rebus or 'Writing with Symbols') can help.

### Signing

Signing (using, for example, Signed English or Paget-Gorman) helps some children and can be used to enhance communication, although rarely is it the main means of communication for a child with speech and language difficulties. It has several purposes:

- as a teaching tool for new concepts or grammatical structures;
- to support the development of reading;
- to give the child a visual prop for the function words in language, e.g. **the**, **is**, **for**;
- to help the child with word retrieval;
- to support comprehension.

Practically, it can be difficult to use signing in a mainstream setting in a meaningful way, although if a child requires this in order to access the curriculum, arguably school staff have a responsibility to develop the necessary skills. Many children who potentially could be helped by signing can and do manage without it. In the absence of signing, teachers simply being aware of the use of natural gesture to support communication can help. The most useful gestures are those that are clear and consistently linked with particular words or structures, for example gestures always linked with 'listen' and 'look', and hand signs used with mathematical words like 'add' and 'take away' which can then also be used with 'plus' and 'minus'. It is important for the class teacher to share these visual cues with other staff so they can be used consistently and passed on to the child's next teacher when they change class.

## *Learning through experiences*

Children who have speech and language difficulties learn best when multi-sensory materials and experiences support auditory input. Teachers are familiar with multi-sensory approaches to learning and those familiar techniques are entirely appropriate as long as the child's speech and language difficulties are considered when planning and delivering them. Here are some suggestions to extend those approaches.

- Role play will help children learn, retain new information and understand stories. Even when a child has severe speech and language difficulties they can join in and if they are confident enough to take a speaking role, they should be encouraged in this. Other children will be happy only with a non-speaking part.
- Using mime as a dramatic medium can help the child to learn through associating movement with sounds or words. Young children will enjoy games like Guess the Action or Follow-my-leader.

- Practical activities such as cooking can be used as a way of teaching verbs. PE lessons are another potentially rich source of opportunities to teach verbs in a dynamic way.
- With good advance planning, school trips can be a tremendously effective way of learning for children with speech and language difficulties. Children need:
  - a clear explanation about what will happen during the trip, possibly with a visual timetable for the day;
  - input on key vocabulary before the trip;
  - modified worksheets, especially if they are to be filled in during the day;
  - ways of 'capturing' key experiences which can then be used as reminders back at school (e.g. a 'goody' bag to collect objects found at the seaside or in the country, a camera or video to record things seen);
  - immediate opportunities for follow-up work, supported by the materials available.

- Linking speech sounds to signs, e.g. Cued Articulation (Passey, 1993), again gives extra visual and kinaesthetic information to children and could be used with the whole class as phonemes are introduced. The child's SLT could offer advice on whether they might benefit from this.

## Support for specific difficulties

This section describes the second strand of support: strategies for specific difficulties. The table shows how the areas covered by the Afasic Checklists relate to the strategies suggested. Having completed an Afasic Checklist for a particular child, simply take the areas of difficulty highlighted by the Summary and then refer to the table to find out which of the following sections in this chapter will be relevant. The strategies should always be implemented with materials and presentation appropriate for the age and stage of the individual child.

Please note that there are no specific suggestions for strategies relating to the section on movement and motor skills. Difficulties in this area can be addressed in PE or by seeking advice from the physiotherapist or occupational therapist.

# Strategies to support specific difficulties

| Difficulties identified | Curriculum areas affected | Children need | Strategies to use | See pages |
|---|---|---|---|---|
| **Checklist 4–5** | | | | |
| **1. Language structure** | | | | |
| Sound articulation | All where spoken or written language is used | • Speech and language therapy<br>• Curriculum adaptation<br>• Specific teaching for reading, writing and spelling<br>• A quiet working environment | • Supporting children who have speech difficulties<br>• Phonological awareness | 45<br>46 |
| Grammar | All where spoken or written language is used | • Specific teaching for reading, writing and spelling | • Working with syntax (grammar) | 55 |
| **2. Language content** | | | | |
| Attention and comprehension | All where spoken or written language is used | • Speech and language therapy<br>• Curriculum adaptation<br>• Specific teaching for all subjects<br>• A quiet working environment | • Good listening<br>• Auditory memory<br>• Classification activities | 41<br>42<br>53 |
| Vocabulary and expressive language | All where spoken or written language is used | • Speech and language therapy<br>• Curriculum adaptation<br>• Specific input for language work and writing<br>• A quiet working environment | • Sequencing<br>• Topic-based vocabulary<br>• Word finding | 41<br>51<br>51 |
| **3. Ability to communicate** | All where there is social interaction | • Speech and language therapy<br>• Social skills training<br>• Structured routines<br>• Small group opportunities<br>• Time for discussions and explanations<br>• A sympathetic working environment | • Wh questions<br>• Social skills and playground strategies | 48<br>49 |

# Strategies to support specific difficulties

| Difficulties identified | Curriculum areas affected | Children need | Strategies to use | See pages |
|---|---|---|---|---|
| **Checklist 6–10** | | | | |
| 1. Response to sound | All where spoken or written language or music is used | • Speech and language therapy<br>• Curriculum adaptation<br>• Specific teaching for reading, writing and spelling<br>• A quiet working environment | • Good listening | 41 |
| 2. Movement and motor skills | All where fine or gross motor skills are used | • Occupational therapy or physiotherapy assessment<br>• Curriculum adaptation<br>• Specific teaching in PE and handwriting<br>• A sympathetic learning environment | | |
| 3. Cognitive processes | All where spoken or written language is used | • Speech and language therapy<br>• Curriculum adaptation<br>• Specific teaching for all subjects<br>• A quiet working environment | • Sequencing<br>• Auditory memory<br>• Written language<br>• Numeracy | 41<br>42<br>43<br>44 |
| 4. Errors in sound | All where spoken or written language is used | • Speech and language therapy<br>• Curriculum adaptation<br>• Specific teaching for reading, writing and spelling<br>• A quiet working environment | • Supporting children who have speech difficulties<br>• Phonological awareness | 45<br>46 |

# Strategies to support specific difficulties

| Difficulties identified | Curriculum areas affected | Children need | Strategies to use | See pages |
|---|---|---|---|---|
| **Checklist 6–10** | | | | |
| 5. Communication | All where spoken or written language is used | • Speech and language therapy<br>• Curriculum adaptation<br>• Specific teaching for all subjects<br>• Social skills training<br>• A sympathetic learning environment | • Salience<br>• Wh questions<br>• Social skills and playground strategies | 48<br>48<br>49 |
| 6. Play and recreation | All where spoken language is used | • Speech and language therapy<br>• Curriculum adaptation<br>• Opportunities for supervised small groups<br>• Specific teaching for reading<br>• A sympathetic learning environment | • Social skills and playground strategies | 49 |
| 7. Vocabulary and<br>8. Grammar | All where spoken or written language is used | • Speech and language therapy<br>• Curriculum adaptation<br>• Specific teaching for language work and writing<br>• A quiet working environment | • Topic-based vocabulary<br>• Word finding<br>• Classification activities<br>• Using idiomatic language<br>• Working with syntax (grammar) | 51<br>51<br>53<br>54<br>55 |

## *Good listening*

Listening properly to each other is the linchpin for successful communication in every situation from a one-to-one conversation to assembly. In the classroom the entire process of teaching depends on children listening to the teacher and taking in information that is primarily auditory. While this process may be supported by visual materials, concepts are introduced 'through the ears'. Children who have speech and language difficulties may need to be taught how to become good listeners.

Good, or 'active' listening involves several elements:

- Good sitting. This means having all four chair legs flat on the floor, hands in lap or resting on the table, sitting up with your back against the chair back. ('Your ears work better when your feet are flat on the floor!')
- Good looking. Look at the person talking. This allows you to see their facial expression and gestures to support understanding of what is being said.
- Good thinking. This involves making associations, checking you understand, trying to note mentally and remember important details.

These ideas need to be discussed and explained to children and then explicitly reinforced. For example:

*'I noticed Adam was being a good listener – he was sitting well and looking at me.'*

Children will enjoy playing games to encourage good listening. Try to vary the type of auditory input by using, for example, musical instruments, spoken instructions, stories and environmental sounds.

POINTERS

**Listening games**

- Simon says;
- I went to market and I bought . . . ;
- Find the hidden ticking timer;
- Walk or run to the (changing) beat of a drum;
- Follow whispered instructions;
- Listen for the deliberate mistake in a poem, story or list.

## *Sequencing*

Children are often described as having 'difficulties with sequencing'. This is an area of difficulty that has many different aspects, manifests itself in various situations and impacts across the curriculum. For example, a child may have difficulties with:

- word order in sentences;
- retelling stories and events;
- describing a series of actions in a science experiment or DT task;
- temporal sequencing – e.g. before/after, morning/afternoon;
- rote sequences such as days of the week, the alphabet;
- following a sequence of instructions.

Here are some suggestions to help in tasks that have sequential elements.

- Teach children the meaning of common sequential 'markers'. These include words and phrases such as **first**, **and then** and **last**. Relate these to games involving following instructions:
  *'Jenny, it's your turn.* ***First*** *clap your hands* ***and then*** *stand up.'*
  *'Hannah,* ***first*** *jump in the blue hoop* ***and then*** *sit on the mat.'*

1

2

3

4

'What happened *before* she fell off the swing?'

'What did her dad do *after* she fell off the swing?'

Use the same language in relation to everyday instructions in the classroom:

*'**First** I want you all to tidy your maths away **and then** sit on the carpet.'*

- Do story sequences using a series of published cards or the children's own pictures. Change the number of pictures to increase or decrease the complexity of the task.
- Demonstrate a sequence of actions (or do an activity like cooking). Draw pictures of what you did and then sequence them.
- Cut up written sentences and re-order them so they make sense. Do the same thing with sentences from a story.
- Display a timeline in the classroom relating to the current week. Mark both regular and special events. You could also do this for a single day using a timetable written on a whiteboard or use a calendar to show a whole month or year. Use the timeframe appropriate for the child and be consistent in referring to it and using it.
- Learn rote sequences in small chunks with plenty of repetition and revision.
- Teach time vocabulary in a systematic way. Concepts such as 'before' and 'after' are difficult because they change according to the period of time you are referring to. Start with concrete examples (e.g. picture sequences). Target understanding of the words and then use of them.

## *Auditory memory*

Children with speech and language difficulties, almost without exception, have problems with short-term auditory memory. This is the kind of memory we use when we are told a telephone number and need to hold it just long enough to dial it, or when we remember a spoken instruction just long enough to carry it out. If we hear something enough over time, we assign it to long-term memory (we 'learn' it). In the classroom, the implications of poor short-term auditory memory for the child are significant.

- The child will have difficulty in following instructions, especially if they are long or complex.
- They will find it hard to learn rote sequences (days of the week, the alphabet, tables etc.).
- Their vocabulary development will be affected because they will need to hear new words more often in order to learn them.

The most effective way to help the child is to support them in developing strategies to manage their limited memory skills. Our aim is to enable the child to cope independently but also to modify our delivery of language while they are still in the process of developing their independence. Here are some ideas.

- Always ensure that you have the child's full attention before giving instructions in order to maximise their chances of taking in what you are saying.
- 'Chunk' information into manageable bits and check the child has understood at each stage.
- Use visual support for auditory tasks.

- Use natural gesture or signs to support instructions.
- Teach the child to use strategies such as saying 'I don't understand' or 'Please can you say it again'. (Ensure that all adults in the classroom are aware that this is a strategy you are encouraging.)
- Encourage the child to use rehearsal, i.e. repetition of what they have heard.
- Help the child to develop a recording system, e.g. drawing pictures of what they have to do to help them remember details and sequence. An older child could try writing notes.
- Encourage use of visualisation ('make a picture in your mind').
- Encourage the child to pay attention in situations that are primarily auditory, such as assembly. Direct their attention, e.g. 'I want you to remember at least two things that Mrs Jones talks about today.'

There is, as always, a balance to be struck between giving the child 'just enough' support but not so much that they become dependent on the adults around. Remember too that if the child feels under pressure to respond, their memory difficulties may become worse. Playing memory games is a good way of stretching memory skills in a relaxed situation.

**POINTERS**

**Memory games**

- Twenty Questions;
- I went to market and I bought . . . ;
- Give or follow instructions for an obstacle course;
- Listen for a word in a story; respond with an action.

## *Written language*

Speech and language difficulties may have a major impact on the development of written language skills. Mature reading, writing and spelling are based on a complex interaction between phonology, semantics, syntax and motor skills that are held together by pragmatic and world knowledge. Disruptions in processing may make production of written work problematic. Here are some suggestions to support children as they develop these skills.

- Ensure that the child clearly understands the task.
- Talk the task through with the child before they start. This could include discussing significant events, writing out key words and reminding them which tense they are using.
- Think about time constraints. It may take the child much longer than the rest of the class to produce a piece of writing because they will need extra thinking time. You may need to allow them more time to do the work, or to reduce the amount of work they are required to produce (e.g. one page instead of two).
- Think about the purpose of the writing and whether the task could be modifed. Is it a language task in which the child has to produce a piece of creative writing? Or is it a recording task (e.g. in science) which they could have an adult to scribe for them? Could they use a worksheet and just write in key words?
- If the child finds spelling the most difficult aspect of the writing task, what do they find helpful? Can they use a wordbook? Can they use 'magic lines'? (e.g. if they were stuck for the word **donkey** they might write **d_____** or **d__k__** in the first draft. This would be checked and completed working with an adult on a final draft.)

| Who? | What did they do? |
|---|---|
| | |
| **Where?** | **What happened next?** |
| | |

- Give the child a framework for the task – e.g using **wh** questions as a (visual) prompt. **Who** is the story about? **Where** are they? **What** happens? Writing frames can provide extra structure and visual support for writing activities.
- Ensure that the child understands the idea of 'beginning', 'middle' and 'end' in relation to a story or description of events.
- Use pictures as a way of helping the child maintain the focus of the work.
- Some children respond well to colour coding as a way of helping them to structure sentences – e.g. nouns are underlined in red and verbs are underlined in orange. Using this system, coloured lines can be drawn and the child can then construct their own sentences using the given syntax.
- Give the child sentences that need to be ordered correctly to tell a story.
- In a small group take turns to add a sentence to a story (either written or spoken).
- Give the child a piece of written work and ask them to find all the errors you have made (based on errors that they typically make).

### *Numeracy*

Mathematical skills are concerned with number but they are also concerned with language. For this reason, children who have speech and language difficulties may experience considerable problems in acquiring mathematical skills.

The language of maths describes number and space and time, so it is both abstract and relational. The development of mathematical skills calls upon all language processing skills. Children with speech and language difficulties may therefore have a variety of obstacles to progress in maths. Here are a few examples.

- Poor vocabulary will affect understanding of specific words and concepts – e.g. how do you interpret an instruction such as 'Colour all the shapes apart from the triangles' if you hear 'apart' as 'a part'? Given your short-term auditory memory problems as well, you might easily interpret the instruction as 'Colour a part of the triangles.'
- Phonological processing difficulties can make discrimination of similar-sounding words problematic – e.g. the difference between 'thirteen' and 'thirty' may be difficult to detect.
- Word-finding problems may affect recall of number names and shapes. Thus it may appear that the child does not know the answer to a question when in fact they are simply stuck for the word or have made a naming error – e.g. calling a triangle a 'rectangle'.
- Motor problems may affect recording skills, in terms both of learning how to write legible numbers and of organising written work on a page.
- Motor/spatial difficulties may affect practical skills such as being able to use a ruler or systematically count counters.

- Temporal (e.g. **before/after**) and comparative (**more/less**, **some/all**) vocabulary may present difficulties because relationships are not the same in every circumstance.
- The fact that several different words may be used to refer to the same mathematical operation can cause considerable confusion – e.g. **minus**, **take away**, **subtract** and **how many left**? (To complicate matters, 'take-away' is also a type of food and 'left' is something to do with 'right' – which also means 'correct'.)
- Some children will find it difficult to generalise concepts and language from one type of task to another, or to recognise that they have already met a particular concept or word in a different context.
- Mental maths can be a particular kind of nightmare for children with speech and language difficulties. This is because it requires children to process complex language and then hold on to the words long enough to perform abstract mathematical operations before giving a verbal reply.

add
plus
more
sum
altogether

–

take away
minus
subtract
less

times
multiply
lots of
groups of
sets of

Strategies for supporting children in numeracy are the same as the strategies you use in other curriculum areas, but there is even more emphasis on visual support and experiential learning. You will find that repetition is essential for concepts to be learned, understood and retained. Here are some ideas that may help.

- Wherever possible, give the child support apparatus – e.g. a number line or blocks for counting. They may continue to need apparatus for much longer than their peers.
- Give the child small targets – e.g. when learning the 4-times table, ask the child to learn the first three facts rather than all ten, and then give extra time for checking they have retained this before you move on to the next stage.
- Give support for the child's motor skill – e.g. if the task is to do with recording sums but their number writing is poor, see if they could do it using numbers already written on stickers.
- Use cue cards to help them remember and learn mathematical operations.
- Show the child what terms mean and use a multi-sensory approach whenever possible – e.g if teaching **more than**, use several different types of materials and contexts and reinforce them frequently across curriculum areas.

## *Supporting children who have speech difficulties*

Children who present with difficulties in speech production may have very different underlying processing skills. For this reason, correction of speech production is best left alone unless you are following advice given specifically by the SLT for an individual child. However, there are some general principles that may be helpful (see also What do I do when … ? on page 55):

- Always listen carefully to the child and show that you value their contributions to discussions and conversation.
- Even if the child's speech is hard to understand, it is possible to shape situations in such a way as to maximise your chances of following what they are saying – e.g. you can ensure you understand the context for what the

child is talking about; you can ask relevant questions where you already know the answer (not always the best way of developing language skills, but helpful in this situation); you can give alternatives where you can match the child's response to a narrow choice of possibilities.

- Give clear models of correct speech – e.g. if the child says, 'I need a darpener' you say, 'You need a *sharpener*? It's on the table.'
- Use one-to-one situations such as reading together to input clear speech models and to point out the written sounds associated with them.
- Consider using a sound–picture scheme to help the child learn and recall individual speech sounds. They may not be able to say 's' in words but they can learn that the sound 'sss' goes with a picture of a snake. If your school doesn't use a particular system it may be helpful to check which system the SLT uses.
- Be aware of the increased risk of the child having difficulties in learning to read and spell.
- Teach phonological awareness skills.

## *Phonological awareness*

Phonological awareness is the ability to think consciously about sounds in words and to use these skills in reading and spelling. When you are considering the skills of an individual child, it can be useful to think about three broad areas:

- the ability to make judgements – e.g. 'Do these two words start with the same sound?'
- the ability to sort – e.g. 'Put all the pictures of things that end in **p** in one pile and things that end in **m** in another.'
- the ability to generate – e.g. 'How many words can you think of that start with **s**?'

There are lots of materials available for working on phonological awareness but it is also helpful to build up your own bank of suitable pictures for different types of activities. Include pictures for:

- CVC words (no consonant clusters);
- one-, two-, three- and four-syllable words for sorting and clapping;
- rhyming words, ideally in sets.

In work on phonological awareness, always remember to be aware of the *sound* rather than the letter. For example, **shop** is a CVC word because it has three sounds (sh-o-p); **giraffe** does not begin with the same sound as **goat** and **circle** starts with the sound 's'. Here are a few activities to develop phonological awareness.

### Segmentation

- Into words:
  - Practise counting the number of words in a sentence or phrase, perhaps

starting with names or nursery rhymes and using the written form as a support to start with. (For young children this activity may be limited by their number skills.)

- Into syllables:
    - Clap each child's name according to the number of syllables in it, e.g. Han-nah, Beth-a-ny.
    - Play games with compound words, 'chopping' them up into their component parts, e.g. **rainbow** is **rain** and **bow** (Can we say 'rainbow' without the 'rain'?).
    - Sort pictures into one, two, three or four syllables. Give children support by clapping words with them if needed, the aim being for them to sort on their own. Use numbered post-boxes or similar props to make this more of a game.

- Within the syllable:
    - Put CVC pictures out on the table. Present the words split into onset and rime, e.g. **c-at**, **b-oat**, and **m-oon**. Ask children to find the picture of the thing you are naming. If they can do this successfully, increase the difficulty by presenting as separate phonemes, e.g. **c-a-t**, **b-oa-t** and **m-oo-n**.

## Single phoneme level

- Initial sounds:
    - Sort pictures (no written clues) by their initial sound. Give support as needed; the aim is to be able to sort independently.
    - Play auditory Odd One Out. Say a list of words and ask the children to listen for one that does not fit – e.g. 'I'm going to say some words that all begin with **b**. Let me know if you hear a word that begins with a different sound. **Bear, Ben, ball, boat, buy, moon, bench**. Good listening! You stopped me on **moon**. What sound does **moon** begin with? That's right, **moon** begins with **m** and we were listening for words beginning with **b.**

- Final sounds:

  Awareness of final sounds and the ability to segment them is a developmentally later skill and should not be introduced until children are secure with initial sound segmentation. Activities can be the same as those used with initial sounds.

## Rhyme

Awareness of rhyme and the enjoyment of playing with sounds begins at pre-school age but the ability to reflect consciously on rhyme comes later. These ideas may help.

- Use poems and nursery rhymes to give children experience of rhyme and encourage them to repeat rhyming words after you. Show them the written words, pointing out the same letters and talk about the end of the words being the same.
- Say pairs of words and ask the children to say whether or not they rhyme – e.g. 'I'm going to say some pairs of words. You listen. Tell me if they rhyme. **Hen**, **ten**. Yes, they rhyme, they've both got **en** on the end. **Cat**, **shoe**. No, they don't rhyme. They have different sounds on the end.'

## *Salience*

Some children seem to have difficulty in judging the relative importance of information and when faced with lots of detail cannot sift through it to decide what is most relevant. For example, when shown a picture of lots of people in a park and asked 'What's happening?', the child may say things like 'He's got a yellow jumper' or 'The bike's got two wheels', rather than 'It's a picture of a park and there's a boy going down a slide.' In retelling a story the child may talk about tiny details and omit the main event. They may also lose the focus of a discussion and begin to talk about irrelevant things.

To help children develop skills in judging salience, it is useful to ask questions such as 'What's the most important thing happening in this picture?' or 'Tell me the three most important things that happened in that chapter.' You may also need to give feedback when the child talks about details that are not important or loses the focus. For example, 'The boy *does* have a yellow jumper but is that important in what is happening?' or 'We are not talking about dinosaurs at the moment because that's nothing to do with this story.' Here are some more ideas for developing these skills:

- Ask children to think of a title for a picture or a chapter of a book. Encourage them to think of one that highlights the most important thing that is depicted or described. Use this approach for 'real-life' events – e.g. when they tell their news, ask them what they would call it if it were a film or a book. For older children, newspapers or magazines can be a valuable source of materials for this kind of activity.
- Summarise events for children using bullet points or numbered lists – e.g. 'Let's think about what we've done this afternoon. We could call it "Monday's literacy hour" and the two main things we did were reading some poetry and writing a poem of our own.' When children are used to this, they could fill in their own sheets that can form the basis of a learning diary.
- Use video clips for the same type of activity, with children watching 10 minutes of video, then working in small groups to decide what the most important events were. Then compare the work of the different groups. (This is also a useful activity for working on comprehension of events.)

## Wh *questions*

Understanding and use of questions can be a particular area of difficulty for many children who have speech and language difficulties. There may be many reasons why a child does not understand or answer a question, for example poor attention, not understanding inference or not having the vocabulary. Sometimes it seems to be a problem with the **wh** word at the start of the question and understanding what it means.

There are many activities to target work on questions. Here are just a few of them:

- Statement or question? Talk to the children about the difference between questions and statements, i.e. asking and telling. Talk about **wh** words and

POINTERS

**wh questions**

- who;
- what;
- where;
- when;
- why;
- (also how and which).

**Who ... ?**

a question about people

**What ... ?**

a question about actions

**Why ... ?**

a question about reasons

**How ... ?**

a question about ways of doing things

how they can act as a signal that a question has been asked. Take turns to say a statement or ask a question; everyone else has to say which it is.

- Use visual symbols to support the teaching of **wh** words and give the children an association for each word. Make some cue cards to use as a prompt. Introduce the words singly or in pairs and leave **which** and **how** (the most advanced words) until the others are established.
- Enlarge the cue cards and have them in a prominent place in the classroom. When you are asking whole-class questions, emphasise the question you are asking and point to the cue card.
- Choose a set of picture cards showing people carrying out a variety of actions. First go through the cards, focusing on **who** is doing the action (use a cue card to support the spoken question). Go through again (or on another occasion), focusing on **what** is happening. Then go through them, changing the question you ask (i.e. either **who** or **what**) and encouraging the children to listen carefully.
- Use a set of cue cards. Take turns to take one off a pile and make up a question starting with the word you pick up. This could be entirely open or you could use a given topic or picture as a basis for the questions – e.g. the first child picks up a card with **who** written on it and asks '**Who** is sitting next to Michael?' The next child picks up a card with **when** on it and asks '**When** is your birthday, Molly?'
- Write out sentences and analyse them, working out which part of the sentence answers a chosen **wh** question (colour coding parts of the sentence and matching that to different coloured questions can be helpful) – e.g.

Amy ate an ice cream in the park this morning.

| | |
|---|---|
| **Who** is this about? | Amy. |
| **What** did she do? | Eat an ice cream. |
| **Where** was she? | In the park. |
| **When** did this happen? | This morning. |

## *Social skills and playground strategies*

Children with speech and language difficulties may find the playground a difficult place. Extra thinking and planning may be required to make breaktime a happy and successful experience. There may be many reasons for the difficulties and some children may have significant behavioural problems associated with their speech and language difficulties. However, problems arise primarily because the time is unstructured and it is not always possible to provide close supervision. Children may be seen as 'naughty' or uncooperative, especially if all staff are not aware of potential problems and why they might arise. Things to look out for include:

- poor social understanding, making it difficult to initiate appropriately or join in with games;
- general social immaturity in relation to their peers;

- being overly physical in social encounters because their language skills are not sufficiently developed to manage verbally;
- persistence of physical, 'rough and tumble' play when other children are using verbally sophisticated, imaginative interactions;
- poor understanding of the rules of games;
- difficulty in developing and using negotiation skills;
- motor problems affecting physical ability in games like football and managing on playground equipment;
- lack of ability to 'read' other children and so avoid trouble;
- being easily led and so getting into trouble.

Children with speech and language difficulties are also vulnerable to being teased or bullied.

The aim is always for these children to gain independence in the playground and for them not to need special consideration at one of the few times of the school day when they may be relatively free from adult support. However, to get to that point, some children may need a carefully staged programme. Here are some strategies that may be worth considering in such a programme.

- Introduce structure by having closer adult supervision – e.g. a TA outside at playtime.
- Introduce a 'buddy' system where one or two other children are asked to play with the child (use this cautiously and thoughtfully).
- Shorten the child's time outside so that they have a little while in the playground but then choose a friend to come inside to do special activities (e.g. construction toys, computer time, drawing and painting), structured by an adult if necessary.
- Develop one or two playtime targets with the child and ensure that these are consistently reinforced.
- Use small groups to talk about the rules of games and to practise them with an adult until the child is sure what to do.
- Give the child simple rules – e.g. 'no hitting' – reinforced by visual prompts if helpful (e.g. a cue card).
- Remind the child about their targets immediately before they go out to play.
- Social skills groups may provide a good forum for discussion and learning about how to handle situations in the playground. This can include how you ask appropriately to join in. Teach the child 'scripts' for situations they find hard.
- Avoid lengthy discussions about feelings until you are sure that they will understand (although talking about and visually representing simple cause and effect can be a way of helping them to develop these skills).
- Avoid **why** questions because this kind of reasoning is often beyond the child's capabilities and may only make difficult situations worse by increasing the child's distress or frustration.

Teasing and bullying can be dealt with in the way you would normally manage them within your school's policy, but you may need to talk to the child in more depth about how they can recognise these and what they should do. You may also have to explain the difference between friendly and unfriendly teasing. You may have to talk to other children about not teasing at all, however kindly it is meant (friendly teasing can be a signal that someone is seen as part of a social group).

You may need to consider training for staff such as lunchtime supervisors who may not otherwise have an understanding of the child's specific difficulties.

If the child has behavioural problems, there will also need to be agreement between staff about what it is reasonable to expect from them. Clearly, some behaviours are never acceptable and it is important to give the child clear guidelines. However, there may be specific targets that allow for some minor things to be ignored ('zero tolerance' can make life difficult for everyone and may also not be sustainable or effective).

## *Topic-based vocabulary*

Effective vocabulary teaching will make an enormous difference to the child's ability to understand and participate fully in topic-based sessions. The child is more likely to retain the words taught if a systematic approach is taken, for example:

- Identify key words for a topic.
- Find pictures or objects to match the key words.
- Introduce key words *before* talking about the topic in detail.
- Use written words *with* the pictures (and signs if appropriate).
- Talk about the pictures, pointing out visually salient information.
- Give extra information about meaning (e.g. associations).
- Allow children opportunities to access semantic information and name items (e.g. clues games).
- Then reinforce in the topic lesson.
- Revise the vocabulary regularly until words are fully established.

POINTERS

**Games to reinforce vocabulary**

- Pelmanism using picture pairs;
- Kim's Game;
- I went to market and I bought . . . ;
- Find pictures of things that go together;
- Find the odd one out from a set of pictures.

## *Word finding*

We all experience word-finding difficulties occasionally, but for children with speech and language difficulties the problems may be frequent and severe, to the extent that their fluency is disturbed and they feel frustrated and disheartened when trying to communicate. Children may show several different sorts of errors:

- slow recall of familiar vocabulary (they may take several seconds to retrieve the word);
- inaccurate naming where a semantically related word is used – e.g. 'table' for 'chair', 'tiger' for 'lion', 'microscope' for 'binoculars';

- sound errors (not related to any speech difficulties they may have) in which part of the target word is retrieved – e.g. 'cove' for 'comb', 'ingo' for 'igloo';
- overuse of 'fillers' such as 'thingy' and 'stuff';
- circumlocution, where they 'talk around' target words but don't actually retrieve them.

The basis of the difficulties is usually related to the child's ability to process accurately the phonology of new words and then to establish and store an accurate phonological representation of the word for retrieval. (It's a bit like searching for something in a filing cabinet if you are not quite sure where you put it – it takes time.)

Improving word-finding skills can take time but there are many strategies that may be helpful. Our ultimate aim is to give the child strategies that they can utilise independently, but this will also take time and maturity.

### Time

Give the child silence and space to think. Discourage other children (and adults) from helping by filling in the word for them unless that is a strategy that they have said they find helpful.

### Offering help

Say 'Are you stuck?' or 'Would you like some help with this word?'

### Cueing

Different children will find different cueing strategies useful. By observation and asking the child what is most helpful, you can implement an individual plan. You could try the following:

- Repeating the sentence the child has just said – e.g. 'So the man was marking out the football . . . ?'
- Phonic cueing. Give the child the first sound of the target word – e.g. when trying to recall the word **pitch,** give the sound 'p'.
- Semantic cueing. Give the child semantic information – e.g. 'the place where you play football'.
- Signing or gesture.

### Overlearning

New vocabulary (or even familiar words that cause difficulty) needs to be taught thoroughly (see Topic-based vocabulary on page 51) and the child will need extra opportunities for hearing and using the words in context. Teach new words systematically. For example, to teach the word dissolve:

- show what it means using sugar and warm water;
- write the word;
- clap it out, **di-ssolve**, and say it;
- give other examples of things that dissolve;

- make a semantic association such as **dis**appear and **dis**solve;
- go through what you have done again in the same session;
- revisit it the next day and then at regular intervals until it is secure.

**Visual support**

Always support new vocabulary learning with the written word (or picture or symbol for younger children). This gives the child a visual pattern for the word which will help in accurate storage and retrieval.

## *Classification activities*

Classification (or categorisation) skills underpin semantic development. Our language system is based on our understanding of the properties of things and how they relate to each other. If we develop children's understanding of how words are related to each other, we will improve their vocabulary and understanding of words and also enable them to learn new words more efficiently.

Here are some ideas:

- Sort objects or pictures into groups. Start at a level appropriate for the child's level of understanding and the vocabulary you wish to teach. For example:
  - things we eat versus things we cannot eat;
  - things we eat versus things we wear;
  - food versus animals;
  - things with wheels versus things without wheels.
- Groups may be specific to a particular subject, for example:
  - maths: shapes with right angles versus shapes without right angles;
  - geography: cities versus countries.

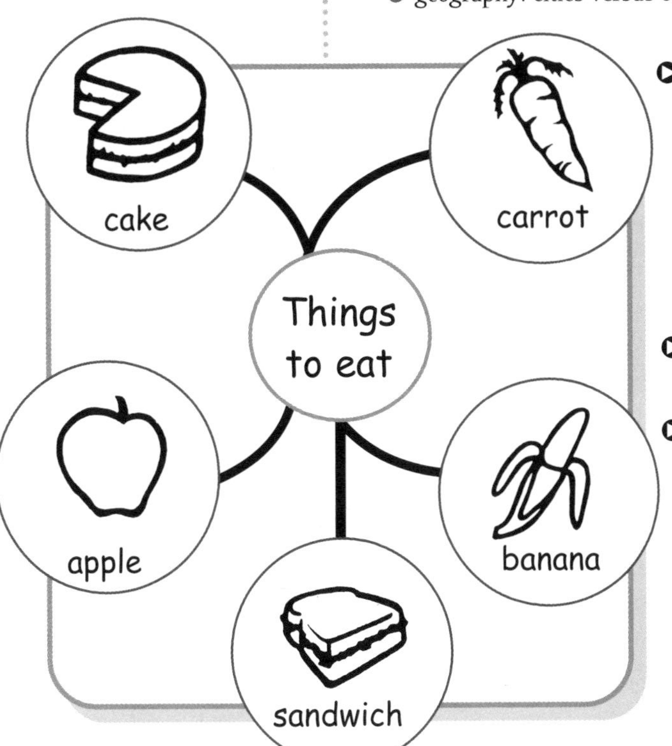


- Odd-one-out tasks reinforce associations – e.g. the child is shown pictures of horse, cow and elephant and asked 'Which one doesn't fit?' Confirm their choices by talking through the explanation, giving support as needed (some children may be able to find the correct associations but be unable to explain verbally).
- Make topic scrap books with associated items stuck in together.
- Give the child a set of pictures and group them according to their semantic features. Then sort the same set in as many different ways as possible using different criteria each time – e.g. animals could be sorted by number of legs, where they live, what they eat, what covers their skin and so on.

- Draw 'semantic circles' to help the child learn new vocabulary and concepts. Do this *with* the child to reinforce learning.
- Support new semantic information by emphasising phonological information – e.g. 'clap' multi-syllabic words, write them down and talk about their sound structure.

## *Using idiomatic language*

Consider the following expressions (taken from a single episode of a popular television soap).

- In the twinkling of an eye.
- She'll get over it.
- It makes me mad.
- Don't get worked up about it.
- She needs a fresh start.
- He'll hit the roof.
- I haven't slept a wink.
- She's riding for a fall.
- That was spot on.

"... and my dad went up the wall!"

Our language is rich in figures of speech – metaphors and similes and colloquial expressions. Children with speech and language difficulties may find it hard to understand what is meant and, unlike other children, may not be able to use the context to work out what we are saying and may lack the confidence to ask. They may also be so used to not understanding that they do not expect to be able to follow. They may simply not listen, especially in large group situations.

This does not mean that we should stop using non-literal language but we should be aware of it and of the need to explain what we mean and check that we have been understood.

There are formal occasions to do this – for example in English where we would teach the meaning of 'metaphor' or 'simile' and find examples in poetry or literature. However, our awareness needs to extend beyond this for children who have particular difficulties in this area.

Here are some ideas:

- Ask the children to watch a particular television programme (you also will need to see it). This could be at home if they understand what they are listening for. You may need to do some research beforehand in order to choose a programme that is suitable for the activity. List all the figures of speech you hear, either in the whole programme or in one part of it. Talk to the children about what they mean.
- Encourage children to identify figures of speech in their reading.
- Choose a 'saying of the week', have it up on the wall and talk about it as opportunities arise.
- Choose four figures of speech and ask the children to include them in a piece of creative writing.
- Make it standard practice to notice examples of figurative language used in any written work done by children.
- Use figures of speech as an assembly topic.

### *Working with syntax (grammar)*

Difficulties with syntax will affect both spoken and written language. The child may sound immature and have difficulty in expressing complex ideas. They may struggle to say complete sentences or have specific problems with particular grammatical structures. The SLT will suggest which structures may be appropriate targets for an individual child.

Here are some ideas to consider:

- Always ensure that the child understands what they are required to say. Check this out in informal activities – e.g. if they do not use the plural **s** (as in **cats**) can they differentiate between the singular and plural by pointing to pictures (of a cat or cats)?
- If the child makes an error in their spoken language, rather than asking them to correct it, feed in the correct model – e.g. if they say 'Dog barking garden', you say 'That's right, the dog is barking in the garden.'
- Plan your target(s) and focus only on the structures you have planned to teach. Ignore other errors if possible – e.g. if your target is pronouns and the child says, 'Him eated my sweets', emphasise the correct word **He**, rather than the word **ate**, asking '*He* ate your sweets?'
- Written work provides an ideal support to reshaping grammatical errors in that the written form of the language stays on the page and can be used for discussion and further practice. Again, targeting the correction is important, especially for a child who makes many errors.
- There is a lot of published material available for teaching grammar. This can provide a good basis for ideas which parents may be interested in using. Be aware, however, that there are rarely enough examples given to allow the child to establish understanding and use of a new structure fully, and you may need to provide further practice materials.

## What do I do when . . . ?

Here are some ideas for dealing with problems commonly encountered when teaching children with speech and language difficulties. Please note that this is not a definitive list and that different children will find some strategies more useful than others. This really is a case of 'first know your child'!

### *The child does not understand what I've said*

- Ask 'Shall I say it again?'
- Repeat the instruction slowly and clearly (but maintaining normal volume and intonation).
- Check the child's understanding of specific words or concepts that may be causing the difficulty.
- Use any relevant visual materials available to support what you are saying.
- Rephrase the instruction or question.

## The child is stuck for a word

- Ask, 'Have you forgotten the word? Would you like some help?'
- Repeat what they have just said to give a lead-in to the word – e.g. 'So, high in the sky you saw a . . . '.
- Ask the child to describe the thing they are thinking of. If necessary, you can repeat this too. 'It's a thing people can go in, it has an engine but not wings, it's got a whirly thing on top and it's like a plane.'
- Ask 'Is it a long word or a short word?'
- Ask 'Can you think of the first sound?'
- Give the child the first sound – e.g. 'I think it starts with an **h**.'
- Once the child has the word, repeat it and ask them to say it again. Reinforce both the phonological and semantic information.

## I can't understand what the child is saying

- Make sure that you are really listening and making the best use of any contextual clues there are – e.g. if they are talking about something in the playground, think 'What *might* it be?'
- Say 'I'm sorry, but I don't understand.' (We often pretend that we understand the child's speech when we do not. Most children are clearly aware of their intelligibility problems and we need to be able to talk to them about this. Obviously this needs to be done with sensitivity and in consultation with parents.)
- Say 'Can you tell me some more about it?'
- See if the child can give you the first sound of any important words. (It is often a single word out of context that is difficult to understand.)
- Sometimes another child may be able to follow what you cannot. Ask the child if it is OK to ask one of their friends to help.
- If all else fails, you may need to say 'I'm sorry, but I'm just not getting this. Can we leave it at the moment?'
- Parents may be able to help if there is a particularly important message that the child wants to tell you.
- Children who are more generally unintelligible can be given successful communication experiences in a variety of ways. In a class discussion, careful use of questions can help – e.g. asking questions that have a predictable answer and giving a choice of two possible answers. In this way the child can be seen to be able to make a valued contribution to what has been said.

## The child makes grammatical errors

- In spoken language you can repeat the correct grammatical structure – e.g. the child says 'My cat catched some mouses' and you say 'Oh dear, he caught some mice!' This can be done in a natural way, which does not interfere with the process of exchanging information but ensures that the child hears the correct structure.
- In written language you could use a straightforward approach, saying 'When there's more than one mouse we say "mice" instead of "mouses".' Write the correct version as a reminder.

- The child's SLT will be able to offer advice about which structures to target in both written and spoken language and also which to ignore – e.g. the child may need to work on pronouns at the moment, but irregular plurals can be left until later.

### *Other children copy or laugh at the way the child talks*

- The solution to this partly depends on the frequency of its happening. A single, one-off comment can be dealt with by a firm 'No, that's not a kind way to behave.' Frequent or persistent comments will need a more concerted approach.
- Talk to the whole class about the fact that we all have things we find easy and things we find difficult. Use a range of examples and ask them for their own ideas. Talk about how it feels to find something difficult and what helps us to feel better. Discuss disabilities including speech and language difficulties.
- Talk directly (not in front of the class) to the children involved. Again stress 'How does it feel?' Perhaps also put this in the context of bullying, if appropriate.
- Talk to the child about what is happening and how they want it dealt with. As in all similar situations, they need to be encouraged to report incidents but they may require more support and time in order to do this effectively.
- Bullying of a child with speech and language difficulties, in terms of management, is no different to any other child and will be seen in the context of the school policy and practice of supporting vulnerable children.

### *The child is socially isolated*

- Look for genuine opportunities to praise the child in front of the class – e.g. 'What a kind thing to do!' or 'I noticed Michael worked very hard on his maths today.'
- Include the child in praise where socially competent and popular children are also named – e.g. 'Sophie, Ibrahim and Michael were particularly good at listening in assembly today.'
- Pair the child with other children who are socially 'on the edge' and look for positive joint experiences (possibly non-verbal activities).
- Include the child in a game or activity with two or three other children which is supervised by an adult to ensure a calm positive atmosphere.
- Any standard activities designed to help with self-esteem can be used to help the child as long as they are adapted if necessary to allow for their communication difficulties.

## Children who have English as a second language

Children who have English as a second language clearly should not be regarded as having a speech and language difficulty. Most children, even if they have had limited exposure to English before going to school, will become competent communicators surprisingly quickly, the development of comprehension tending to precede expressive skills. They will need differentiation in terms of pace and style that accommodates their increasing levels of competency in English. Discussion with specialist teachers will be helpful. However, as with any other group of children, there will be some who do have specific difficulties with speech and language development which may not be identified until they go to nursery or school. Identification of these specific difficulties requires careful observation and the Afasic Checklists provide a framework for this. Children's progress with language acquisition should be closely monitored.

Here are some additional pointers:

- Does the child have difficulties in their first language? This is the critical question to ask, but finding the answer to this relies on setting up a good relationship and effective communication with parents. This may take some time and there are other things to look out for in the meantime.
- Take note of how the child is communicating and with whom. How successful are their attempts?
- Is the child forming appropriate social relationships?
- Is the child's comprehension entirely contextually based or are they able to follow some language which is not entirely 'here and now'?
- What does the child do if they don't understand? What strategies are they using?
- Is the child learning new topic-based vocabulary effectively? (This vocabulary is new to all the children and you might therefore expect their learning to be similar to that of other children.)
- If the child has brothers and sisters in the school, how easily did they learn English?

It is important not to make assumptions about the child's language development until you are sure whether or not it is progressing as you would expect. Obviously, it is also important to ensure equality of access to services such as speech and language therapy and specialist teaching support.

## Outcomes of support

All those involved in supporting children who have speech and language difficulties are, of course, trying to 'make them better'. Some children will indeed catch up with their peers, however, others will not. For them we need to think of support as an ongoing process.

The progress that children make is affected by many different factors. These include:

- the severity of the difficulties;
- the number of speech and language areas affected (e.g. speech, receptive language, vocabulary, syntax).

Children's difficulties may change over time. A child who has speech difficulties may later have reading difficulties, or a child who has mild difficulties in verbal comprehension may later have significant difficulties in text comprehension. Part of our role is to be aware of the changing demands of the curriculum and social expectations and to recognise the signs that the child may be running into problems that were not previously evident. Of course, the opposite may also be the case; children may develop skills and need less support than we anticipate. We need to be alert to the need for decreasing support to allow the child room to develop independence at the right time. The SEN Code of Practice (2001) describes how we might define progress (or 'adequate progress'). It may be progress that:

- closes the attainment gap between the child and their peers;
- prevents the attainment gap growing wider;
- is similar to that of peers starting from the same attainment baseline, but less than the majority of peers;
- matches or betters the child's previous rate of progress;
- ensures full access to the curriculum;
- demonstrates an improvement in self-help, social or personal skills;
- demonstrates improvements in the child's behaviour.

## Target setting and IEPs

We support children by providing an inclusive curriculum. Sometimes it will be enough to differentiate delivery to a level that allows the child to access what is happening in the classroom. For other children this will not be enough. The means of planning for differentiation is the IEP.

The IEP is the tool with which we can plan for the child, provide input and monitor the outcome of our support. When we set targets they need to be:

- small steps;
- measurable;
- progressive.

The process of writing IEPs needs to be integrated into the teacher's general organisation and planning, with time built in for assessment, recording, monitoring and reporting.

The targets should reflect 'what you want to see' and the strategies should reflect 'how you are going to get there'. Inclusion strategies encourage changing the environment to accommodate the child's needs. In order to do that effectively, first we need to describe the child's difficulties. So the planning process needs to work through questions that follow this general order:

① What are the child's strengths and difficulties?

② What intervention shall we provide (the IEP)?

③ What do we do to back up at a whole-class level?

IEPs are best written collaboratively, everyone involved with the child having an input to the process. In fact, IEPs can provide an ideal vehicle for multi-disciplinary planning and discussion. One of the challenges is to make targets functionally useful and to ensure generalisation of new skills. Targets that have been achieved should be routinely checked to ensure that the child has retained and can use newly acquired concepts. Here is an example of an IEP devised for a child with specific difficulties in speech, reading and writing.

Targets should be discussed with children (and devised in collaboration with children to the extent that they are able to manage this). Similarly, children should be encouraged to reflect on their progress.

## Individual Education Plan

| | | | |
|---|---|---|---|
| Name: Robert Wilson | Date of Birth: 20. 3. 96 | Class: Y1 | Stage: 2 |
| Term: Autumn | Teacher: Mr Brignell | Age: 6 | IEP No.: 1 |

General observations:
Robert shows signs of immaturity, specific difficulties in speech, writing and reading, and a lack of concentration in all areas.

<table>
<tr><th>Objectives</th><th>Teaching strategies and resources</th><th>Teaching by whom and frequency</th><th>Success criteria</th></tr>
<tr><td rowspan="5"><u>Literacy</u><br>Robert will:<br>• be able to read and spell 12 new CVC words (cat, dog, in, on, the, is, and, he, we, me, she, was);<br>• read with increasing accuracy;<br>• have consolidated his knowledge of letter sounds.</td><td>Literacy activities with magnetic letters/words</td><td>Class teacher weekly<br>SST weekly</td><td rowspan="5">Robert will:<br>• read and spell the 12 listed words;<br>• read St 4 ORT with 90 % accuracy;<br>• know all of his letter sounds.</td></tr>
<tr><td>Weekly spelling test</td><td></td></tr>
<tr><td>Reading at school and home</td><td>Class teacher weekly<br>LSA weekly</td></tr>
<tr><td>Flash cards of St 3 and 4 words</td><td>SST daily</td></tr>
<tr><td>Phonic games</td><td>SST weekly<br>Extra tuition outside school</td></tr>
<tr><td><u>Numeracy</u><br>Robert will:<br>• know the mathematical language used for 'plus' and 'equals'.</td><td>Revise and use numerical terms</td><td>SST weekly</td><td>Robert will:<br>• be able to give examples of terms for 'plus' and 'equals'.</td></tr>
<tr><td rowspan="2"><u>Self-esteem</u><br>Robert will:<br>• be able to convey a message with 2 parts successfully;<br>• have built self-esteem and confidence.</td><td>Give messages to convey to other staff</td><td>Class teacher daily</td><td rowspan="2">Robert will:<br>• deliver messages successfully and confidently;<br>• show increased confidence and self-esteem.</td></tr>
<tr><td>Read to/with foundation children<br>Set up class computers</td><td>Weekly<br>Weekly</td></tr>
</table>

# Appendix

## The development of the Afasic checklists

### *Checklist 4–5: research background*

Jo Corcoran, David Hiles and David Rowley at the Department of Human Communication, De Montfort University, carried out the development and standardisation of Checklist 4–5. The screening tests were devised in consultation with teachers, psychologists and speech and language therapists. The aim was to provide a reliable and straightforward means of identifying children who had speech and language difficulties who could then be referred for more detailed assessment.

Checklist 4–5 is based on the Bloom and Lahey (1978) descriptive model of language. In this model a distinction is drawn between the following areas:

- language form or structure (sound articulation and grammar);
- language content (attention and comprehension, and vocabulary and expressive language);
- language use (ability to communicate).

In normal language development, these three components are successfully integrated. When language is impaired, there may be isolated impairment of just one component but the overlap between them means that difficulties in one area can have adverse effects on the whole system.

### *Checklist 6–10: research background*

The initial development work on Checklist 6–10 was initiated by Afasic. A panel of professionals worked on the tests and produced a 94-item checklist, divided into eight sections. The rationale for having the different sections was that speech and language abilities do not develop in isolation but in conjunction with other aspects of development.

### *Checklist 4–5: summary of reliability and validity*

Studies were carried out with a total of 59 children in nursery schools in Leicester.

#### Reliability

① A high level of internal reliability has been achieved in Checklist 4–5. Nursery nurses using the checklist achieved a coefficient of 0.955 and nursery teachers, 0.953.

② High levels of inter-tester reliability can be achieved using Checklist 4–5. The scores of nine out of ten pairs were correlated between $r = 0.831$ and $r = 0.989$.

#### Validity

① Checklist 4–5 can discriminate between a group of children attending speech and language therapy and a group of children with no known speech and language difficulties.

② Using a total score of 35, the levels of sensitivity and specificity are 70 per cent and 91 per cent respectively.

③ Using a sound articulation score of 5, the levels of sensitivity and specificity are 94 per cent and 97 per cent respectively.

④ The sound articulation cut-off score may also be able to identify children with both speech and language difficulties and also children with specific speech difficulties.

⑤ The total cut-off score may also be able to identify children with both speech and language difficulties and possibly children with specific language difficulties.

⑥ Although the sound articulation subsection appears to be extremely effective at identifying children in need of speech and language therapy, it is felt to be premature to recommend that Checklist 4–5 consists only of this subsection. Further research is required to investigate exactly what types of problem the sound articulation subsection and the whole test can identify.

### *Checklist 6–10: summary of reliability and validity*

A study was carried out with 240 children from language units and 268 primary-age controls.

#### Reliability

① The research conducted on Checklist 6–10 has focused on the internal reliability of the test. No assessment of inter-tester or test–retest reliability has been carried out.

② In stage 2 of the study, the internal reliability coefficient using Cronbach's coefficient alpha was 0.910.

③ In stage 3 the internal reliability coefficient calculated using Cronbach's coefficient alpha was 0.956.

#### Validity

① The test was able to discriminate between children with known speech and language difficulties and children with no known speech and language difficulties.

② For each of the age groups tested, children with speech and language difficulties scored significantly lower than children with no speech and language difficulties in all eight of the subsections as well as in the overall total.

③ It was found that using a total score of 10 or above, the levels of sensitivity and specificity were 87 per cent and 88 per cent respectively. Using this cut-off score, 87 per cent of the experimental and 88 per cent of the control group were accurately and correctly identified by Checklist 6–10.

# Resources

## Suggested reading

The following lists contain suggestions for books that may be useful if you wish to find out more about a particular area.

### *Speech and language difficulties*

Afasic (1997) *Afasic Glossary Sheets.*

Byers Brown B and Edwards S M (1989) *Developmental Disorders of Language.* London: Whurr

Cantwell D and Baker L (1987) *Developmental Speech and Language Disorders.* The Guilford Press

Fletcher P and Hall D (1992) *Specific Speech and Language Disorders in Children.* London: Whurr

Goodyer I in Bishop D V M and Leonard L (2000) *Speech and Language Impairment in Children.* Psychology Press

### *Supporting children with speech and language difficulties in the classroom*

Martin D (2000) *Teaching Children with Speech and Language Difficulties.* David Fulton

Merrit D and Culatta B (1998) *Language Intervention in the Classroom.* Singular Publishing Group

Ripley K, Barrett J and Fleming P (2001) *Inclusion for Children with Speech and Language Impairments.* David Fulton

### *Guidance and legislation from statutory bodies and the voluntary sector*

DfEE (2000) *Provision of Speech and Language Therapy Services to Children with Special Educational Needs (England).* Report of the Working Group

DfEE Publications (1998) 'Children with Special Educational Needs' in *The National Literacy Strategy.*

DfES (2001) *Inclusive Schooling: Children with Special Educational Needs.* DfEE 0100/2000)

DfES Publications (2001) *SEN Toolkit.*

DfES Publications (2001) *Special Educational Needs Code of Practice.* (DfES 581/2001)

ICAN (2001) *The Joint Professional Development Framework.*

### *Useful advice on strategies*

Johnson M (1992) *Functional Communication in the Classroom: A Handbook for Teachers and Therapists of Language Impaired Children.* Manchester Metropolitan University: Clinical Communication Materials, Department of Psychology and Speech Pathology

Johnson M (1997) 'Lost in a moving stream: auditory sequential memory deficits' in *Speech and Language Therapy in Practice.* Winter 1997, Avril Nicoll

Rinaldi W *Social Use of Language Programme.* NFER-Nelson

Gorrie B and Parkinson E (1995) *Phonological Awareness Procedure.* STASS

### *Specific approaches*

Passey J (1993) *Cued Articulation.* STASS

Rebus Symbols: *Writing with Symbols 2000.* Widgit Software Ltd.

Paget-Gorman Signed Speech: various publications are available from STASS

### *Support materials*

There are many excellent published resources for supporting speech and language difficulties. The following list is by no means exhaustive.

#### LDA

*Chatter Boxes*
A selection of LDA language materials collected together with activity cards for use by TAs. Includes additional resources such as counters, spinners and bean bags to facilitate playing a wide range of games.

*Things that Go Together* and *Opposites*
Puzzle cards for semantic association and expressive language work.

*Sound Beginnings Rhyme and Alliteration Picture Cards*
Flexible material for phonological processing games.

*Action Lotto*
Single and composite pictures showing actions around the house. Useful for a variety of expressive and receptive language tasks.

#### Taskmaster

*Preposition Overlays*
Facilitates dynamic and interactive teaching of prepositions.

*Category Cards*
Attractive cards showing common categories for semantic work.

# References

## STASS

*Semantic Links*
Useful, carefully graded semantic material.

*Semantic Connections*
Comprehensive categorisation cards that can be used for a wide range of activities.

## Winslow

*Colour Cards*
Beautiful photographic cards providing essential resources for language work.

*Pragmatic/Semantic Speech Bubbles*
Great fun and very useful for expressive language, social understanding and verbal reasoning skills.

## *Organisations*

## Afasic

Afasic is the UK charity which supports children and young people with speech and language impairments and their parents or carers. They also provide support and information to the professionals. Their services include support through national and regional development officers, a helpline dealing with all aspects of speech and language impairments, courses and training, and numerous publications.

Afasic
50–52 Great Sutton Street
London EC1V 0DJ
Phone: 020 7490 9410

Email: info@afasic.org.uk
www.afasic.org.uk

Helpline: 0845 3 55 55 77 (local call rate; open Monday to Friday. 10.30am - 2.30pm)

## References


Bishop (1992) 'Biological basis of developmental language disorders' in Fletcher P and Hall D (1992) *Specific Speech and Language Disorders in Children*. London: Whurr

Bloom L and Lahey M (1978) *Language Development and Language Disorders*. New York: John Wiley and Sons

Byers Brown B and Edwards S M (1989) *Developmental Disorders of Language*. London: Whurr

Cantwell D and Baker L (1987) *Developmental Speech and Language Disorders*. The Guilford Press

Goodyer I in Bishop D V M and Leonard L (2000) *Speech and Language Impairment in Children*. Psychology Press

Passey J (1993) *Cued Articulation*. STASS

# Glossary

**Articulation**: the physical production of speech sounds.

**Attention**: the ability to focus in an appropriately sustained way on a particular task or activity. Where a child is unable to do this at the level expected for their age, they may be described as 'distractible'.

**Auditory discrimination**: the ability to recognise and distinguish similarities and differences between speech sounds.

**Auditory memory** (sometimes called short-term auditory memory): the ability to process and retain heard information. The 'short-term' label implies that the kind of memory required is like that used to remember a new telephone number. It must be held in the mind long enough to be able to dial it, but there is then no further need to recall it, unless it is a number that needs to be learnt. In this case, it is committed to long-term memory through repetition. Short-term auditory memory skills are needed in the classroom for things like following instructions.

**Developmental dysphasia**: used by some authors to refer to developmental language disorders; the term is now less common than it used to be. Dysphasia and aphasia refer to the loss of some or all language as a result of acquired brain damage through stroke or head injury, for example.

**Disordered pragmatic skill or development**: see Pragmatics.

**Dysarthria**: motor speech difficulties affecting the accuracy and power of muscle movements (so that speech sounds slurred).

**Dyspraxia**: motor speech difficulties affecting the planning and co-ordination of muscle movements.

**Language processing**: the system that enables spoken words to be perceived, stored and interpreted, and also enables thoughts to be encoded and produced as speech.

**Makaton**: a sign system based on a structured approach to teaching vocabulary.

**Morphology**: grammatical elements that affect meaning – e.g. plural **s** (**cats**), past tense **ed** (**walked**).

**Phonological processing**: the ability to discriminate between and manipulate speech sounds. Children may have phonological difficulties or disorders affecting speech production.

**Phonology**: the rule-based system of sounds used in speech.

**Pragmatics**: the rules about how we use the language that we have in social communication. Disordered pragmatic skill or development means that a child has difficulties in understanding and using the rules of interaction in an appropriate and flexible way.

**Receptive language**: understanding what is said.

**School Action**: interventions, agreed by the SENCo and class teacher, that are additional to or different from those provided as part of the school's usual differentiated curriculum.

**School Action Plus**: interventions provided by external specialists or services that are additional to those provided by School Action.

**Semantics**: the meaning of words.

**Syntax**: the structures we use to put words together into sentences (grammar).